# Agile Reimagined

## Building Mindsets for Smart Delivery

Nancy Juneja



ARCCHIE
www.arcchieonline.com

# Agile Reimagined

## Building Mindsets for Smart Delivery



**Editor**: Shambhu
**Production Manager**: Gaurav Mutreja
**Cover design by** Freepik and Vecteezy
**Formatting & Indexing:** Rahul

First Edition: Jul-2025
Reference: 2303274
Published by Arcchie Publications

ISBN-13 (paperback): 978-8198698124

Published by ARCCHIE PUBLICATIONS, Greater Noida, U.P. -201 306
and Printed at Repro India Ltd., Mumbai

*www.arcchieonline.com*

## JOIN US ON THE ARCCHIE PUBLICATIONS DISCORD SERVER

Connect with fellow readers, authors, and enthusiasts to discuss all things related to our publications and the exciting world of AI, programming, and learning. Share your insights, ask questions, and engage in vibrant discussions to expand your knowledge and inspire creativity. Take advantage of this opportunity to be part of a dynamic community dedicated to exploring the frontiers of technology and innovation. Join our Discord Server today and be part of the ARCCHIE Publications community!

***https://discord.gg/z26SenmpEt***

# DISCLAIMER

The information contained in this book is for educational and informational purposes only. While the publisher and authors have made every effort to ensure the accuracy and completeness of the information provided, they assume no responsibility for any errors, omissions, or contrary interpretation of the subject matter contained herein. This publication is sold with the understanding that the publisher and authors are not engaged in rendering legal, accounting, or other professional services. If legal or expert assistance is required, the services of a competent professional should be sought. Any trademarks, service marks, product names, or named features are assumed to be the property of their respective owners and are used only for reference. There is no implied endorsement if we use one of these terms. The views and opinions expressed in this book are those of the authors and do not necessarily reflect the official policy or position of any agency, organization, employer, or company. The publisher does not warrant the performance, effectiveness, or applicability of any sites listed or linked to in the book.

# ABOUT THE AUTHOR

**Dr. Nancy Juneja** is the Founder and CEO of Revup Life Skills, Co-founder of MENTORx Global, and Director General at LUCR8 Ventures. Recognized with the prestigious Karmaveer Chakra by the United Nations, she has received over 350 awards for her contributions to education and entrepreneurship, including Educationist of the Year (five consecutive years) and the Women Achievers Lifetime Achievement Award. Coming from a family with a legacy of running educational institutions in Delhi for over three decades, Dr. Juneja is a Mentor of Change with NITI Aayog, Government of India, and serves as an Advisor to the United Nations Peacekeeping Forces Health Emergencies Program and the World Health Organization. She actively mentors startups as a Business Blaster Coach with the Government of NCT Delhi and as a mentor under the StartUp India Maarg initiative. A seasoned edu-leader and peak performance mentor, Dr. Juneja has over 20 years of industry experience guiding students, startups, and corporate leaders across strategic and operational roles. She is a three-time TEDx speaker, holds a Ph.D. in Psychology and Business Management from the USA, and has authored 12 books and numerous international research papers. Her contributions have been recognized with two Indian patents and world records in the Guinness Book of World Records and Scholar's Book of World Records.

# ABOUT THE TECHNICAL REVIEWER

**Dr. Gaurav Aroraa** is a distinguished Microsoft MVP award recipient and an influential Regional Mentor of Change with AIM NITI Aayog, Government of India. He is a Business Coach and innovation Leader with Business Blaster, Government of NCT Delhi, and he contributes significantly to the startup ecosystem. Dr. Aroraa is a lifetime Computer Society of India (CSI) member. He holds certifications as a Scrum Trainer and Coach, ITIL-F, PRINCE-F, and PRINCE-P, showcasing his expertise in project management and IT service management. Dr. Aroraa is an accomplished open-source developer and an active contributor to the Microsoft TechNet community. With a rich background in technology, he has authored books across diverse fields, addressing both emerging and established technologies. His recent achievements include being recognized as a world record holder for his contributions to books in exceptional and cutting-edge technologies. Dr. Aroraa inspires professionals, educators, and students through knowledge-sharing initiatives and mentorship.

# PREFACE

In today's dynamic world, adaptability and speed are no longer optional – they are survival skills. Agile Reimagined: Thriving with Smart Deliveries in the AI-Driven Era is designed for professionals, leaders, students, and enthusiasts who want to understand not just the mechanics of Agile but also the mindset that unlocks its full potential. This book takes you on a journey from the traditional approaches that once ruled software development to the transformative power of Agile practices. It clarifies what Agile truly means, dismantles common misconceptions, and demonstrates how Agile thinking is reshaping industries beyond IT. As organisations step into an AI-driven future, the ability to integrate emerging technologies like Generative AI with Agile practices will define who leads and who lags. This book introduces practical, real-world strategies, tools, and case studies to help you not just do Agile, but be Agile – embracing continuous learning, innovation, and customer-centric delivery as a way of life. You're invited to explore these chapters with an open mind, challenge old paradigms, and reimagine your work, team, and organisation for sustainable success.

Let's embark on this journey of learning together.

## What's Inside This Book

**Chapter 1: Rethinking Traditional Software Development** explores how software development has evolved, why structured models like Waterfall and V-Model dominated early practices, their strengths, and the limitations that led to the rise of Agile approaches.

**Chapter 2: Demystifying Agile: Principles and Evolution** explains what Agile truly means, its historical evolution, popular methodologies such as Scrum and Kanban, the differences between Agile and Scrum, and the key roles that enable Agile teams to thrive.

**Chapter 3: Why Agile Wins: Benefits, Limitations, and Hybrid Approaches** Learn how Agile addresses core challenges in traditional SDLC, its apparent benefits, potential drawbacks, and how hybrid models combine Agile with structured approaches to tackle complex, real-world projects.

**Chapter 4: Cultivating an Agile Mindset** Discover the core characteristics of an Agile mindset, the "Four Cs of Agile" (Collaboration, Communication, Commitment, Continuous Improvement), and practical ways to build an Agile culture in your team or organisation.

**Chapter 5: Leading Successful Agile Transformations** Gain insights into designing and executing Agile transformation strategies, developing T-shaped skills for team versatility, and managing resistance to change during Agile adoption initiatives.

**Chapter 6: Choosing the Right Agile Framework** Dive deep into leading Agile frameworks, their strengths, use cases, and a structured approach to selecting the best-fit framework for your team, project, and organisational goals.

**Chapter 7: Agile Across Domains: IT and Beyond** explores how Agile practices benefit not only IT projects but also non-IT domains like marketing, HR, education, and operations, with practical examples of Agile applications and common challenges in diverse sectors.

## For Whom This Book Is Intended

This book is ideal for:

- Students studying software development, project management, or business analysis who want a clear introduction to Agile concepts.
- Professionals are moving into Agile roles such as Scrum Master, Product Owner, or Agile Project Manager for the first time.
- Team members working in IT or non-IT environments want to understand how Agile can improve their daily work.
- Managers and leaders seeking practical knowledge to guide their teams through Agile practices and transformations.
- Anyone curious about how Agile works and how its principles can be applied effectively in different industries.

## Errata

At **ARCCHIE Publications**, we are committed to delivering the highest-quality content in all our publications. We follow best practices to ensure the accuracy of our content to provide our readers with indulgent reading experience. We believe and understand that our readers are our best judges, and we always use their input and feedback from time to time to improve human errors, if any, that may occur during the publishing processes involved. We invite you to participate in our errata submission process to ensure our books remain accurate and up to date. Please help us reach out to readers who might have difficulties due to unforeseen errors. Please write to us at ***errata@arcchieonline.com***.

When submitting errata, please include the following information:
Book Title, Reference#, Author(s), Page Number, Description of the Error, Suggested Correction (if applicable)

The **ARCCHIE Publications** Family highly appreciates your support, suggestions, and feedback.

## Sharing Your Perspective and Providing Feedback

Your perspective is invaluable to us, as it helps us enhance our content and gather your feedback. We warmly welcome all forms of feedback. Please feel free to send us an email at **feedback@arcchieonline.com**, mentioning the book title in the subject line of your message.

## Book Review Invitation

We kindly invite you to share your thoughts. After you've read and engaged with this book, consider leaving a review on the platform where you acquired it. Your impartial feedback can greatly assist potential readers in making informed decisions. Your reviews provide valuable insights for us at **Arcchie**, helping us better understand your perspectives on our products, and they offer authors the chance to appreciate your feedback on their work.

## Piracy

Should you encounter unauthorized reproductions of our publications in any digital format on the internet, we kindly request your assistance in pinpointing their locations or website sources. Please reach out to us at **copyright@arcchieonline.com** and include a link to the infringing material.

If you possess expertise in a particular subject and wish to participate in the creation or contribution to a book, please visit ***authors.arcchieonline.com***. We welcome you and assist you to start your authorship journey with **ARCCHIE PUBLICATIONS**.

# TABLE OF CONTENTS

# 1

# Rethinking Traditional Software Development

In the current era of evolving Software development, it is essential to journey back to the roots of our craft to appreciate how far we have come. This chapter delves into the foundation of software development, exploring the traditional approaches that have shaped the industry for decades. From the very early days of waterfall methodologies to the more structured and linear processes. We will unravel the principles, practices, and challenges associated with the traditional approach to software development. By understanding where we began, we can better comprehend the leaps and bounds of our progress and appreciate the need for innovative methodologies that have emerged in response to the complexities of modern software projects. Join us as we embark on a retrospective journey through time, exploring the tried-and-true methods that continue to influence and inform how we build software today.

In this chapter we will discuss:

- Understanding Software Development Life Cycle (SDLC)
- Need for Software Development Life Cycle (SDLC)
- Different Models -Waterfall Model, Incremental Model, Spiral Model, V Model, etc.
- A downgrade of the traditional model.

**Understanding Software Development Life Cycle (SDLC)**

In 1960, SDLC started to become a formal process for software development. SDLC is a structured, cost-effective, and time-efficient process to enable the production of high-quality software in the shortest possible time. SDLC aims to design, develop, and maintain a superior application that meets customer expectations. SDLC outlines – Detailed plan, stages/phases which we can measure, and this, in turn, will enhance the speed of development and minimize the project risks and effort & and cost wastages.

The way technology is changing nowadays, Software development is a challenging area to manage. SDLC provides a systematic management framework with deliverables at every stage. We will discuss the various stages of traditional and agile software development.

Here are some advantages of Software Development Life Cycle (SDLC):

- Clear segregation of duties (SOD) among different teams & individuals, e.g., developers, tes- ters, business analysts, Project Managers, and Client Project Managers & Business team. SOD documents have details on the responsibilities of developers, testers etc. Developer has responsibil- ity of development and unit testing and testing and tester has responsibility of system testing, integration testing and performance testing. Generally, there should not be overlapping between respon- sibilities and different roles. In this case tester should not have responsibility of unit testing and developer should not have responsibility of system or performance testing.
- Visibility of all processes for all stakeholders
- Scientific and proven estimation, planning, and execution of projects.
- Better risk management along with mitigation processes
- Defined communication channels between all stakeholders.
- We defined exit criteria at each step/process.

**Phases of SDLC**

The Software Development Life Cycle (SDLC) typically consists of seven phases. These phases ensure that the software is well-planned, developed, tested, deployed, and maintained effectively. Here are the seven phases of the SDLC:

1. **Project Planning** – Planning is the first phase of software development. It has a vital role in the software delivery lifecycle, where the team estimates the cost and defines the requirements of the new application. The planning may contain several steps; this step's outcome is a Project Planning document. There is a very popular saying in the IT industry – "If you cannot plan, then you will not be able to deliver." The first phase of SDLC is crucial and will build a strong foundation for our end goal.
2. **Requirement Gathering** - Generally, Business analysts for the application domain collect the requirements from customers and convert them into functional requirement documents for developers. These documents will bridge the gap between the customer and the technical team.
3. **Design** – In this phase, architects from the project build the application's design, keeping all aspects in mind, be it hardware sizing, software licensing, volumetric of the application, etc. Generally, the team presents one or more options to build the application, and post-approval from the client, the final approach can be taken forward.
4. **Development/Coding** – This is the most significant phase of SDLC. The development team builds the code for the application using the technology stack defined during the planning and design phase. In this phase, the majority of the team gets involved in building the application. The developer team will do the

actual coding and often take help from the business analyst/ architect team to understand the requirements clearly.

5. **Testing** – The development team completes the unit testing when developing the application and after successful development and unit testing. The application will be deployed in a test environment for overall testing, whether system, integration, or load testing.
6. **Deployment** – Post successful system, integration, load, and user acceptance testing; finally, the application will get deployed in the production environment by the DevOps team for all user access.
7. **Maintenance** – This is the final step of SDLC, where the development team hands over the application to the maintenance team to handle bugs or minor enhancements in the application.

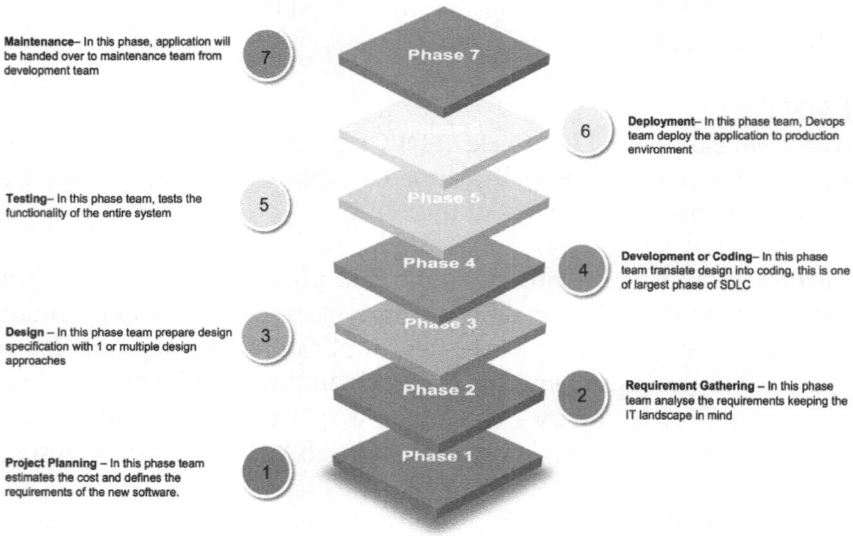


*Figure 1.1 – Seven Phases of Software Development Life Cycle*

**Need of SDLC**

SDLC is the methodology for all stakeholders involved in software development; the IT Project Manager mainly tracks this. Phase-wise delivery will give a client a bird eye view of the overall software development process.

**Note**: *PM stands for Project Manager. A Project Manager is an individual responsible for planning, executing, and overseeing a project from its initiation to completion. Their role includes defining project goals, managing resources, and ensuring that the project is completed on time and within budget.*

SDLC helps PM to track the signoffs/approvals systematically; multiple signoffs are required on each phase of SDLC. We can call this the Exit criteria of each phase; fulfilling the exit criteria for a phase is necessary for the team to move to the next phase. This will help avoid issues during later stages, e.g., in case some issues come post-Go-Live, and the development team has been put on the spot for this mistake. It is a task of the PM to find the root cause of this issue and who shares the signoff to move ahead with development, whether it is missing from the developer, Team leader or tester or functionality was built as per requirement shared & signed off by the customer. It is not the main motive to pinpoint the team or person responsible for the issue but to take learning from the same and incorporate the missing process in the SDLC cycle.

Every phase of SDLC has exit criteria; below are details for a few phases:

- **Requirement phase** - The team builds the requirement document and gets it reviewed and approved by the client. Sign-off on the Requirement document is the exit criteria for the re- quirement phase; with approval, next phase ideally should be started. Design Phase – Team prepares the design document for Architect approvals, whether client or account Architects. Exit criteria for this phase is approval from Architects.
- **Development Phase** – The team will perform the development from the design document and take it forward with the Team leader for review and sign-off.
- **Testing Phase** – The testing team performs the system and integration testing and shares their final sign-off for User acceptance testing. In User acceptance testing, the business users will perform the testing on the application and share their final sign-off for production deployment.

**SDLC Models**

Software Development Life Cycle (SDLC) is a structured approach to managing software development projects. It defines the various stages involved in developing a software application, from the initial planning and requirements gathering to the final deployment and maintenance. There are different SDLC models, each with its own unique approach. Each model follows a series of phases, such as requirements gathering, design, development, testing, and deployment.

Various SDLC models are available for software development, and each model has pros and cons. The model selection depends on the organization's approach or specific customer approach to handling software development.

**Waterfall Model**

It has seven phases, which has been explained in Figure 1.1 It is a sequential development process and flow from top to down as waterfall. Every phase has set exit criteria, and the next phase will not get started till the previous phase is not complete. This offers less flexibility to move back to the previous phase in case any issue is identified during a later stage. The time and cost of moving back to the previous phase are generally very high as the same phase needs to be completed again for the changes initiated during a later stage, e.g., when the testing team finds an issue in a workflow pattern. Workflow is getting stuck in circle and needs to move out to next step in a specific scenario. The requirement of the same has been identified during the requirement phase, then this needs to go back to the requirement phase where the business analyst needs to update the requirement document and get it signed off by the client. Post signoff complete cycle repeats for this functionality - redevelopment (Keeping a watch already developed functionality should not get impacted), complete unit testing and retesting. These changes at a later stage will come under the change management process, and apart from the impact on the delivery timeline, they can also impact on the project's cost. All stakeholders need to be agreed to the proposed changes and impact on time & cost. Even a small change during a later stage has a considerable impact and will go through long change management processes and approval. There are various features of waterfall model and its very interesting to know the details on this feature.

Below are the details for your reference:

- **Sequential in Nature** - Follow linear approach in delivery.
- **More emphasis on detailed documentation** - Each phase needs to deliver a set of documents to move to the next phase of the model.
- **Limited customer interaction** - The customer business team gets involved in the first requirement-gathering and user acceptance testing phases. In between, all phases revolved around the IT team only: business analysts, developers, testers, or architects.
- **Upfront high-level planning** - It requires high level planning during starting of project and refinement at start of each phase.
- **Lack Agility** - It lacks agility to accommodate any changes during any phase. Each feedback or change must go through a long process and development cycle.
- **Best for stable IT project environments** - This is best suited to the IT landscape where there are no changes in requirements and allows the team to deliver the project with the exact requirements, which was shared maybe 3 or 6 months or 1 year back. This is best suited to de- liver compliance requirement, which generally does not change drastically.

Waterfall is suitable for all kind of software development project but here is the list of project where it is best suited

- **Small scale projects** - Project where scope is simple & well defined.
- **Compliance projects** - Generally, regulatory compliance has defined requirements which was thought through by government officials and went through a government process before they were shared with the industry. Significant asks from these requirements are solid documentations and artefacts at each level. Waterfall model is best suited for these compliance projects.
- **Legacy system** - Waterfall is best suited where requirements are from legacy systems

or in- frastructure e.g., Mainframe, AIX or iSeries etc.

**Increment Model**

In this model, software is being developed in various iterations/increments. Every increment will develop the partial or minor functionality of the overall project. Each increment passes through multiple phases. The following are the phases of Increment model:

- **Requirement Gathering** - Generally, requirements are gathered into small groups de- pending on priority and dependency to work as standalone functionality, e.g., In the case of the development of Customer Relationship Management (CRM) software, the first group can be divided into functionality that focuses on customer-facing functionalities and backend functionalities, or reporting can be delivered in next increment.
- **Design & Development** - In this phase team focuses on design & development of a current increment.
- **Testing** - The testing team performs system and integration testing for the current and pre- viously delivered increments to avoid any negative impact on running functionality. Post suc- cessful testing, increment will be released to pre-production environment for user acceptance testing

Broadly, all these phases will be repeated in each increment till all defined increments are delivered to production. The proceeding Figure 1.2 depicts the increment model and the phases in each increment. Every increment has additional feature of overall product. Combining Increment1, 2 and 3 makes the product complete as per business needs.

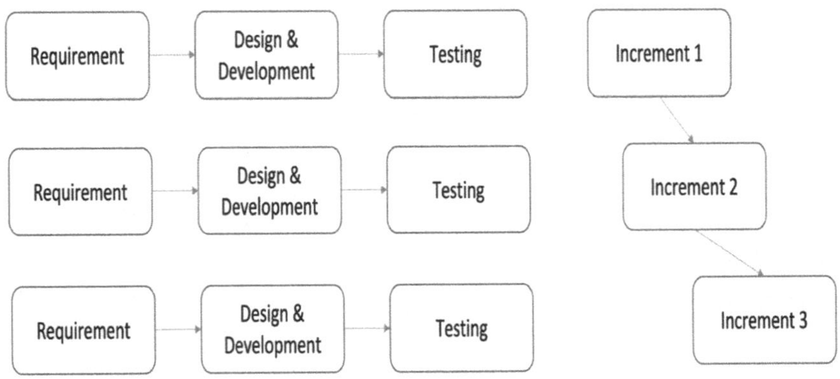


*Figure 1.2: Increment Model*

**Spiral Model**

This model is an amalgamation of the waterfall and increment models, focusing more on risk management. It allows increment development, incorporating client feedback, and mitigating risk at each phase of the cycle. The phase of the spiral model has 4 quadrants, as depicted in the proceeding Figure 1.3.

The Spiral Model has the following phases:

- **Requirement gathering & planning** – This phase gathers requirements from the client and elaborates. Alternative solutions can also be proposed during this phase.
- **Risk Analysis** – In this quadrant, all solutions and associated risks are brainstormed. Pos- sible risk mitigation will be proposed in this phase, and the final approach will be selected for development.
- **Development** – In this quadrant, selected solution is being developed and testing for final delivery.
- **Next Phase Planning** – In this quadrant client share feedback on developed product and any shortcoming or changes for the same. Along with changes, planning for the next phase is initiated in this phase.

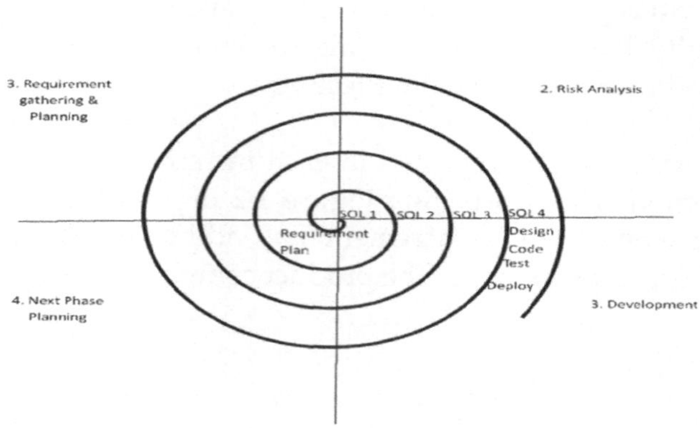


*Figure 1.3: Spiral Model*

**V Model**

It's also called Verification and validation model as its more focused on testing on each phase. This is best suited for a project where teams are not collocated. Figure 1.4 shows the process where development/coding sits on the base of V and rest of phases form the V. The V-Model, or Verification and Validation model, is a software development and testing methodology that follows a sequential approach, with each stage of development accompanied by a corresponding stage of testing. This model emphasizes the early detection and correction of defects, as well as ensuring that the software meets the expectations of the end-users or customers.

**Verification Phase**

The V-Model's verification phase stresses early defect detection and correction, preventing issues from spreading to later stages of the development life cycle. It aims to catch problems as soon as possible, ensuring that the software meets the specified requirements and design.

- **Requirement Gathering** - Team gathers and elaborate client requirements.
- **System Analysis** - The team analyzes the requirement and prepares a system analysis document.
- **Design** - In this phase team creates high- & low-level design.
- **Development** - In this phase team code the application using specification shared in high & low-level design.

**Validation Phase**

The validation phase is essential for ensuring that the software works as intended and satisfies the quality standards set during the required phase. It involves various types of testing that together provide confidence in the software's accuracy, performance, and security. Successful completion of the validation phase indicates that the software is ready to be released to the end-users or customers.

- **Unit testing** - In this phase, the team develop a test plan and test for the smallest unit of code, and generally developer do this kind of testing.
- **Integration testing** - In this phase, the team focuses on integration testing, which means testing across different modules and validating that the application works independently and with all across modules, be it an internal or external application module.
- **User Acceptance testing** - In this phase, the customer business team tests their requirement and finally share sign-off for deployment.

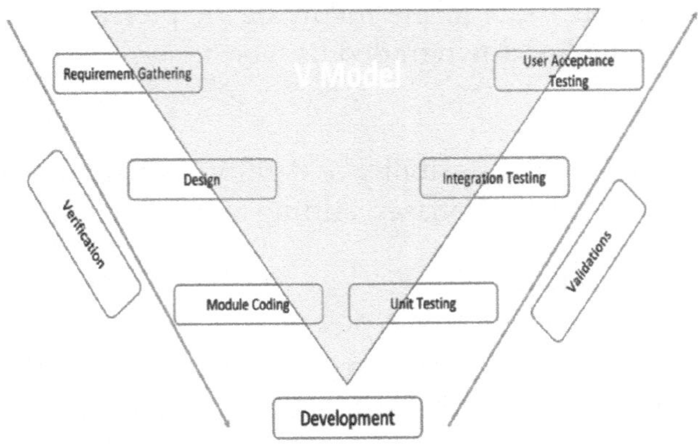


*Figure 1.4: V Model*

**Waterfall Versus Incremental Versus Spiral Model**

We have learnt about major SDLC models, below is the brief difference between Waterfall, Incremental and Spiral model.

| | Waterfall | Incremental | Spiral |
|---|---|---|---|
| Approach | Sequential | Incremental | Incremental with focus on risk management |
| Flexibility | Low | Medium | High |
| Risk | High | Low | Low |
| Detailed Documentations | Required | Required but less than waterfall model | Required but less than waterfall model |
| MVP Availability | No | Yes | Yes |
| Client Involvement | Less | Medium | Medium |
| Team Size | Large | Mid-Size | Mid-Size |
| Ease of Use | Yes, Simple | Yes, Simple | Complex |

*Table 1.1: Difference between Waterfall, Incremental & Spiral*

**Downgrade of traditional Models**

Every model has its own life, and with time, things evolve. Best solution of past becomes irrelevant in the future due to various changes in the process. The same philosophy fits in for SDLC as well. With rapid change in technologies & process, software development needs a model which can adopt and dash. Many things could be improved in the traditional model, which has started a new era for the Agile model; you will learn more about Agile in the following chapters. Let us discuss why the traditional model has failed or downgraded its worth:

**Fixed Processes**

Traditional models have limited flexibility or Agility, and team needs to follow rigid linear process. Post-completion of phases, adding any new changes or feedback from customers is challenging.

**Limited Feedback Mechanism**

Customer feedback has been taken at the initial phase, i.e., during requirement gathering or at the final stage of the project. This leads to unsatisfied customers once they see the final product during the last stage of the project, i.e., user acceptance testing.

**Late identification of issues**

Only after the final development of the entire product will the application be released to the testing team for their system/integration testing. This results in a potential delay in finding the bugs or requirement gaps, and the cost of this delay is costly in terms of cost and time.

**Requirement Misalignment**
In the traditional model, requirements are signed off during the initial stage and considered accurate from all aspects, which is not the correct assumption for long-duration projects. There are lots of jokes on the internet where the client has given the requirement of an animal with four legs, one tail, and a fat belly this customer means an elephant, but what was delivered at the end of the development is Buffalo. Now you can understand what all it will cost to convert the buffalo to elephant.

**Process-oriented Change Management**
First, it was tough to convince customers they missed the requirement during the first phase, and now it's an additional requirement. Once it is agreed as an additional requirement, it will go through all phases again, starting from requirement gathering and cost in a big way financially and in the delivery timeline.

## Summary

Now let's recap what we have learnt in this Chapter

- Understanding of SDLC - This chapter delves into the foundation of software development, exploring the traditional approaches that have shaped the industry for decades. SDLC is a structured, cost-effective, and time-efficient process to enable the production of high-quality software in the shortest possible time. SDLC aims to design, develop, and maintain a superior application that meets customer expectations. SDLC outlines – Detailed plan, stages/phases which we can measure, and this, in turn, will enhance the speed of development and minimize the project risks and effort & and cost wastages
- Maintenance Need of SDLC - We need SDLC because it is a structured and systematic approach to software development that helps to ensure that the software is developed on time, within budget, and to the required quality standards.
- Different type SDLC Models – Waterfall, Incremental, Spiral & V Model

In the next chapter, we will explore SDLC Model as the next step:

- What is Agile and how does it evolve?
- Users will get an understanding of Agile methodologies.

# 2

# Demystifying Agile: Principles and Evolution

The IT industry has always had a focus on managing and development of software in the best possible way. Through the past few decades, several approaches have been explored and experimented with. Agile is the result of such experimentation, strengthened with intense practice, and made flexible with the freedom to explore. However, it is interesting to note that Agile as a methodology is not just relevant to the IT industry but also other industries where the key focus is customer satisfaction. In fact, some of the frameworks in Agile have found their origin in other industries like manufacturing, Marketing, HR etc. Let us explore the world of Agile further.

This chapter will cover:

- Evolution of Agile
- Agile Manifesto
- The need for Agile
- Agile Key concepts
- Agile Frameworks
- Agile Methodologies
- Agile Roles
- Agile Ceremonies

**Evolution of Agile**

Every industry needs a method for madness. To streamline the working, processes are created, and methodologies are built. These methodologies enable some amount of consistency in the way the industry operates. They also provide guidance on how to work towards achieving an end goal. The IT Industry has also created many different methodologies to build software. The Waterfall Model is one of the oldest models. This model is also frequently used to introduce the Software Development Lifecycle to a professional. The primitive Software Development Lifecycle assumed a big-bang approach to building software. It also made several assumptions and to some extent resisted change. However, the industry soon saw that change was the only constant. To operate in such an environment of change and dynamism, there was a need for a methodology that was robust enough to handle the destructive nature of change. This led to creation of the Agile Method of working.

***Note:*** *In the year 2001, a team of 17 software developers got together to create a set of guiding principles which came to be known as the Agile Manifesto. This historic moment took place in a ski resort at Snowbird, Utah. Visit http://agilemanifesto.org/history.html to learn more interesting facts about Agile Alliance and the creation of the Agile Manifesto.*

The word 'agile' means ability to move quickly and easily. However, the word 'Agile' got re-defined in a completely new way with the advent of Information Technology to deliver services to clients in a fast and the most effective manner. The term 'Agile' was coined by the Agile Alliance to represent the guiding principles that
embody the Agile Manifesto.

**Agile Manifesto**

Created and signed by the seventeen software development practitioners, the Agile Manifesto is a set of guiding principles and methodologies for today's Agile software development. In the context of software development, Agile simply characterizes adaptability, flexibility and responsiveness to change in software development.

The Agile Manifesto lays emphasis upon the following set of values:

1. Individuals and interactions over process and tools
2. Working software over comprehensive documentation
3. Customer collaboration over contract negotiation
4. Responding to change over following a plan

The above values can be realized by an iterative and incremental approach for project management. This approach leaves room for feedback and improvement. It is characterized by mini development cycles that give the developer and the client an opportunity to visualize the outcome, improvise upon it and keep adding features to it until the complete software or product is ready.

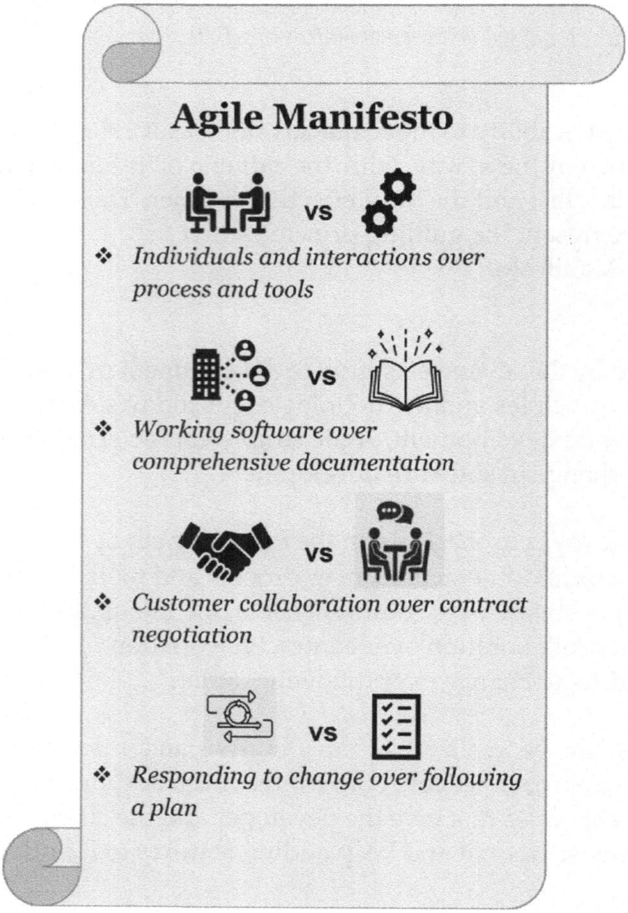


*Figure 2.1: The Agile Manifesto*

There are 12 important principles behind the Agile Manifesto that help in realizing the value of Agile. The principles are listed below:

***Our highest priority is to satisfy the customer through the early and continuous delivery of valuable software.***

An agile team is highly focused on ensuring customer satisfaction. It achieves this by having the customer perform interim spot checks as the team builds the working software iteratively.

Early feedback helps to validate the functionality in advance, thus making sure that the team is proceeding in the right direction, and there are no surprises later.

***Welcome changing requirements, even late in development. Agile processes harness change for the customer's competitive advantage.***

While agile teams focus on showing a working software to the customer, they are also open to receiving feedback that may result in tweaking or changing the requirement itself. A working software helps the customer to envision the end result better. In this process, if there is a change required to make sure the end result aligns perfectly with the vision that the customer has, the team is proactive to adopt the change and work its way forward to deliver.

***Deliver working software frequently, from a couple of weeks to a couple of months, with a preference to the shorter timescale.***

Showing a working software gives the opportunity to show progress and build confidence with the customer. It also ensures that there are no changes at a later stage since the customer gets a chance to see the working software and is enabled to provide early feedback, which may sometimes result in a change.

***Business people and developers must work together daily throughout the project.***

Business people are one of the key stakeholders as they know the requirement best. When the development team creates a working software, the business team is able to check if it aligns well with the expected functionality to be able to address the needs of the end user. Hence it is important that the developers always collaborate with the business team.

***Build projects around motivated individuals. Give them the environment and support they need, and trust them to get the job done.***

Agile believes in self organizing and self-directed teams without the need to micro manage each activity. A team that decides what it will deliver, delivers it best! The organization just needs to ensure that the dependencies are met and there are no bottlenecks.

***The most efficient and effective method of conveying information to and within a development team is face-to-face conversation.***

Agile recommends having co-located teams that shares a common workplace and interacts face to face. This helps to increase their productivity, resolve dependencies faster and avoid any communication gaps.

***Working software is the primary measure of progress.***
A working software best describes the requirements that have been implemented. Hence it is the best measure of progress.

***Agile processes promote sustainable development. The sponsors, developers, and users should be able to maintain a constant pace indefinitely.***

The ability to maintain a constant pace is only possible if there is continuous support provided to the team, impediments are resolved on time and the customer has focus and commitment to validate and approve working functionality. This ensures that all stakeholders are committed towards the end objective.

***Continuous attention to technical excellence and good design enhances agility.***

Attention to technical excellence ensures minimal impediments, and hence a swift progress. A good design is the foundation for a stable and resilient outcome. These characteristics together ensure that agility is enhanced.

***Simplicity–the art of maximizing the amount of work not done–is essential.***

Maximizing the work not done ensures that nothing falls through the gaps and all the work is planned into the development cycle and tracked to completion.

***The best architectures, requirements, and designs emerge from self-organizing teams.***

A self-organizing team has complete freedom to be flexible and agile, to enhance the design and architecture based on the outcome. Often if the team is not self-organizing, they have dependencies on multiple stakeholders, some of whom may not be directly connected with the project. In such circumstances, the pressure to abide by all stakeholders often results in compromising the design. This is not the case in agile.

***At regular intervals, the team reflects on how to become more effective, then tunes and adjusts its behavior accordingly.***

**Tip:** *Self-reflection helps the team to retrospect on their previous actions and brainstorm on what improvements could lead to a better experience. This helps in ensuring continuous improvement.*

## The need for Agile

Before Agile came to be defined as a way of software development, software was usually developed in a Waterfall Model. This meant that software was developed in stages, following a rigid and well-defined path, starting from Requirement Gathering and Analysis, Design, Development, Testing and Deployment. Each of the stages in the Waterfall model is sequential and follows a fixed order. The output of one stage becomes the input for the next stage. Hence it is imperative that the stages be followed through sequentially. It was impossible to jump any stage. If something went wrong during any of the stages or did not turn out to be as per expectation, it was discovered only during the Testing stage. These discoveries got classified as defects. These defects were fed back to the development team which fixed the defect in the Design or Code, followed by unit testing, integration testing and so on. Finally, when the software was found to be defect-free, it was shipped to the client. The client tested the software and identified defects, if any, and fed them back to the development team. These defects again followed the same path of fix-test-deploy. As a result, the finished and defect-free product took very long to reach the client (or market). This long wait was often not good for business!

Agile is the answer to the problems caused by the waterfall model. As clearly called out in the Agile Manifesto, the Agile methodology solved the following incumbent problems that the erstwhile Software Development Life Cycle (Waterfall Model) failed to address:

- Elaborate processes and tools distract software developers from the end objective Often elaborate processes present a bottleneck to the development team as it interferes the work of a developer who has to keep going back and forth between code and documentation to make sure they are in synch. To support elaborate processes, there are equally elaborate project management tools that require frequent intervention into the developers work to keep them up to date. Agile emphasizes upon usage of only those processes and tools that add value to the end-product. If a process is not enhancing the value of the end-product, it is not needed. An agile team does not require fancy tools to collaborate. Agile teams are usually co-located, quick to interact with each other and have a visual representation of the work and its progress in front of them. However, it is definitely also possible for distributed teams to adopt Agile. Various collaboration tools assist remote teams in adopting Agile easily. (The pandemic in 2020 is an excellent example when various agile teams across the globe collaborated successfully). In Agile way of working, we generally create a team which has a flat structure as opposed to the hierarchy in a typical waterfall model, which enables individuals to interact freely. The Technical Manager encourages healthy interaction and removes any bottlenecks to communication.
- Lengthy and comprehensive documentation is not easy to maintain. Lengthy and comprehensive project documentation is not just time taking to create, but equally cumbersome to maintain. It requires careful and dedicated personnel to continuously update the documentation as the project progresses. Teams often lose focus amid rework, struggle to meet timelines and client expectation. The first work product that takes a hit in such situations is documentation. The end result is a set of documents which do not align with the delivered product. An attempt to update such documentation is not only time taking, but also futile as it adds no value to the product. A Technical Manager focusses on the work- ing software over comprehensive documentation!

However, it is not entirely right to say that there is zero documentation in an Agile Project. The Agile team carefully decides upon the optimal required documentation to make the software deliverable complete.

- **Complex contract negotiation is not synonymous with client satisfaction** Unlike the Waterfall model, where the contract is complicated and negotiated hard to make sure nothing slips through the cracks, eventually leading to a rigid and non-satisfying way of working, an Agile team collaborates and co-creates with the client, continuously showing and telling the client what has been created, seeking feedback and fine tuning the software to meet the clients' expectations. In the non-Agile world, any deviation from the pre-defined require- ments triggers an elaborate Change Management procedure, re-negotiation and re-writing of the contract. Stringent and rigid project plans result in longer time to market. A Waterfall model usually follows a typical lifecycle process by the book. However, a big-bang sequential plan may not always work, especially when requirements are not firmed up and evolve as the team proceeds. Often clients are aware of their business end goal but not sure of how to achieve them. Here is where an Agile project team would come up with an iterative, incremental approach of building the software. This entails delivering value to the customer in short, frequent cycles (known as Sprint), continuously collaborating with cross-functional teams. An Agile team helps the client to gradually realize and define the requirements of the end-product. The above challenges led to the industry getting transformed in various ways while adopting Agile way of working. Organic growth in the Agile era led to teams getting skilled and enabled to performed Agile roles. Further, these Agile enabled teams brought in a combination of technical skills that acted as a catalyst to the transformation of the multi-skilled Agile teams. It also led to an optimized way of working as managers got enabled in Agile and brought elements of their experience into the Agile way of working.

**Agile at play in nature**

Let us try to examine our surroundings and discover traces of Agile in nature and its evolution!

***Exercise your mind***

*Everywhere in the universe, we have seen the Agile methodology at play – be it evolution of the earth or that of humankind. Hence it is quite logical for software also to evolve incrementally. Agile should have been the most natural way of working. However, software development brought in what is known as the Waterfall model first.*

*Think about possible reasons why this may have happened, and why this model stayed on for a long period of time.*

- *Following a sequential development lifecycle gave some time for the team to be on- boarded*
- *A sequential approach allowed enough time for the team to understand the requirements better*
- *The market was not very dynamic, requirements remained static over a longer period of time*

- *The industry was resistant to change*

*Think of other plausible reasons for the convincing popularity of Waterfall model in the initial days of software development.*

**Agile Key concepts**

Agile is all about being flexible, adaptive, collaborative and focused on the customer's needs. To be able to embrace Agile successfully as a team, it is important to understand the underlying concepts of Agile.

- **Iterative and Incremental development**: In an Iterative and incremental approach of development, the overall product is broken down into smaller pieces, each being a working unit and independently testable. Development happens incrementally, with each iteration adding to the functionality of the work product developed so far, until all features are added and the product is ready as a whole. Each iteration allows the work product to be inspected, and feedback if any, is incorporated and the work product is adapted till it meets the customer requirement.
- **Customer collaboration**: Agile encourages close collaboration with the customer. The customer actively participates in identifying requirements, prioritizing features, inspecting and providing feedback. This helps the agile team to be able to meet the customer expectation.
- **Embrace and adapt change**: An Agile team is open to accepting any change in priorities, requirements or plans. The team focuses on short term goals, adjusts the plan and adapts the software according to the feedback so that the end product that is created fully satisfies the customer.
- **Self-organizing, cross functional teams**: Self organizing teams collaborate closely and are empowered to take any decisions impacting their goals. They work together, share responsibilities and face any challenges to be able to meet their goal successfully.
- **Continuous improvement**: Continuous improvement is a result of early inspec- tion and adaptation – whether it is the software, or the processes being followed.
- **Accept feedback**: Early validation and verification of work adds multiple feedback loops in the process which helps the team build a product which exactly matches the customer expectation
- **Transparency and visibility**: Agile believes in being transparent, encourages close collaboration and communication with the customer. This helps the team is overcoming any bottleneck in the plan early enough. Complete transparency helps to build trust within the team and with the customer.
- **Working software**: Agile believes in delivering small but testable and working software in each Iteration or Sprint. This enables the team to get early feedback from the customer so that there is an opportunity to adapt the software as per the customer need.
- **Retrospective meeting**: Retrospective is a very significant ceremony in Agile. This

meeting is held at the end of a time-boxed iteration. Often, the meeting hap- pens without the presence of senior management in order to enable free exchange of thoughts. There are three key topics that form the agenda of a retrospective meet- ing – What went well? What did not go well? What could have been better OR what could have been done differently? The outcome of a retrospective meeting is a key lever for improvement of processes and practices in the future iterations.

**Agile Frameworks**

Agile is an umbrella term for several iterative and incremental development approaches, with each of those variations being its own Agile framework. While each Agile framework has its own unique qualities, they all incorporate elements of iterative development and continuous feedback when creating a product. Any Agile development project involves:

- Continuous planning
- Continuous testing
- Continuous integration
- Other forms of continuous development

Each Agile framework is considered lightweight. Rules and practices are kept to a minimum, especially when compared to traditional waterfall-style processes, and are designed to be adaptable to all kinds of circumstances. The focus falls on empowering team members to collaborate and make quick and effective decisions together as a group. The grand vision behind Agile is to create applications in small increments, with each individual increment tested before it is considered complete. This process assures quality is "built" into the product, versus inspecting for quality later.

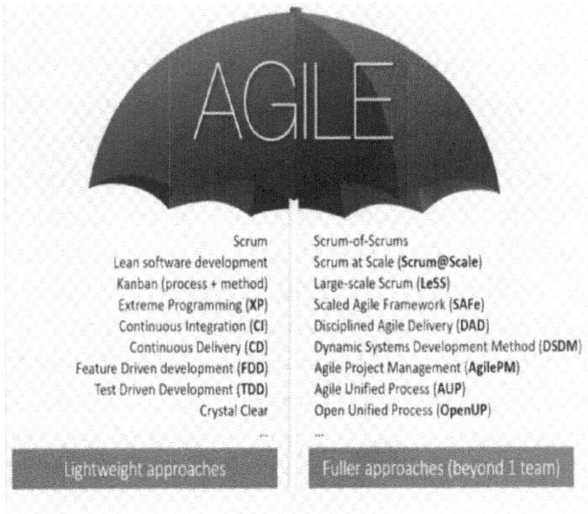


*Figure 2.2: The Agile umbrella (ref: mendix.com/agile-framework)*

Agile and Scrum are terms often used inter-changeably, but it is important to understand the difference between the two. The key difference is that Scrum is a specific framework within the bigger concept of Agile. Agile has a set of values and principles, which Scrum and other Agile methodologies inherit. Hence practitioners often confuse between the two.

- Agile focuses on frequent and early delivery of value to the customer, along with continuous feedback and improvement. On the other hand, Scrum is a more structured approach of managing projects with very specific roles, ceremonies and work products.
- Agile emphasizes upon self-organized, cross-functional teams whose roles may be defined according to the organization's practices. Scrum has very specific roles defined – Scrum Master, Product Owner and development team. Each of these roles have their own well-defined responsibilities.
- Agile has ceremonies or meetings according to the needs of the organization or team, like Backlog Refinement, Retrospective, Demos or Spot checks etc. Scrum has spe- cific ceremonies with well-defined agenda – Sprint planning, daily Scrum, Sprint re- view, Sprint Retrospective.
- Agile has several artifacts or documents that support the framework, like user stories, product backlog, burn-down chart etc. depending on the organization preferences. Scrum has very specific artifacts, each having its own purpose – Product backlog, Sprint backlog, Increments.

## Agile Methodologies

Agile is often described as a methodology, but it's more accurate to refer to it as a set of principles and values for software development. The Agile Manifesto, created in 2001 by a group of software developers, outlines these principles and values. It emphasizes collaboration, customer satisfaction, and flexibility in response to change. Agile is not a strict methodology with a specific set of rules and procedures, like some traditional methodologies (e.g., Waterfall). Instead, it provides a flexible framework for iterative and incremental development. Various methodologies and frameworks have emerged from the Agile principles, including Scrum, Kanban, Extreme Programming (XP), and others. So, while Agile itself is not a detailed methodology, it has given rise to several specific methodologies and frameworks that teams can choose and adapt to their specific needs. These methodologies and frameworks provide more concrete processes and practices for implementing Agile principles in practice.

The key motive of following Agile is to enable flexibility, collaboration, continuous improvement, responsiveness to change and quality outcomes. To achieve these motives, the team applies an incremental and iterative approach to software development and project management. An Agile team consists of members with cross-functional skills, is self-organizing and self-directed. Hence, the team is quick to embrace change and adapts itself easily. Agile teams generally have better collaboration with the client, thereby promoting high customer satisfaction. There are several Agile methodologies - some more popular amongst Agile teams and other lesser-known ones. Here are some of the popular Agile methodologies:

### Scrum

Scrum is one of the most widely known frameworks of Agile. For someone who is not well versed with concepts of Agile, this is often mistaken to be like traditional Project Management. However, Scrum is very different from traditional Project Management.

A traditional Project Manager usually plans the execution of the complete project in one go. The Project Plan starts with the Inception stage and goes on until closure of the project. However, Scrum works very differently. In a Scrum, the project is divided into multiple smaller cycles, usually up to 4 weeks in duration. This short cycle is referred to as Sprint or Sprint Cycle. This mechanism of breaking down the product into smaller chunks is very useful when the product is complex. It helps the team to understand the Product and build it bottom up, gradually. The overall requirements or features (unique pieces of functionality) are added to the Product Backlog. A Product Backlog is a listing of all the requirements, including defects, and is the single place where the complete product requirement is kept. This list or backlog is owned and managed by the Product Owner. A Product Owner is an important role in Scrum and is responsible for maintaining and prioritizing the product backlog.

The Product Owner nominates the prioritized features from the backlog (based on technical and business priorities) into the Sprint. The person who facilitates this short cycle is called the Scrum Master. It is common for a Tech Manager to slip into this role once (s)he learns the concept of Scrum, and develops the mindset to facilitate and coach the team rather than direct. The Scrum Master is a key role in this methodology and is responsible to ensure that the Scrum Team is making progress. The Scrum team comprises of the Scrum Master, the Product Owner and the Development Team which is cross-functional, self-organizing and self-directing. The Scrum Master acts as a coach whose primary responsibility is to ensure that the team is clear about the scope of the sprint and all the pre-requisites and dependencies for implementing the scope are met on time. In case there is any bottleneck, it is the responsibility of the Scrum Master to ensure it is taken care of, and the team can continue working without any disruptions. Agile defines various ceremonies (or meetings) for the team to function effectively. An important ceremony which the Scrum Master is responsible to facilitate, is the Daily Scrum or Stand-up meeting. The frequency of this meeting is usually daily, each meeting typically runs for not more than 15mins. It is imperative that the meeting duration be controlled to ensure that the team adheres to the agenda strictly. In these 15 minutes, the team shares what they have accomplished since the last meeting, what they plan to do next and whether there are any impediments. A disciplined Agile team often holds the Scrum meeting or the stand-up meeting in standing position in their workspace. At the beginning of each Sprint, the Scrum team does the planning in a Sprint Planning meeting. They collectively define the Sprint Goal and identify items from the Product Backlog to be worked upon in that Sprint.

At the end of each Sprint, a Sprint Review meeting is held where the completed deliverable is show-cased. This presents an opportunity to rest of the team to share feedback and adapt the product. After the Sprint Review, the Sprint Retrospective is held in which the entire team joins and shares their experience in terms of what went well, what did not go well, and what could have been done differently. Feedback from the Sprint retrospective is fed into the next sprint. The key essence of Scrum is to be flexible, respond to change early, realize value early by inspecting and adapting, and ultimately lead to better customer satisfaction and better value realization.

*Figure 2.3: Foundation, 3 Pillars and Values of Scrum*

**Kanban**

Kanban is another popularly embraced Agile methodology that focuses on visualization of progress of the work done. A Kanban board helps to visually depict the progress of work. The board is typically divided into stages – To do, In Progress and Done. An Agile team is free to add in other relevant stages that can help them monitor progress.

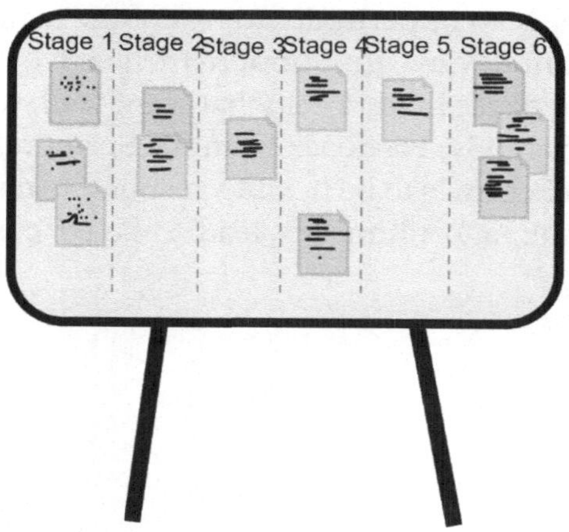


*Figure 2.4: A Kanban Board*

Each work item, task or user story is depicted on a Kanban Card or a sticky note. It has a short description of the task, due-date and assignee. The Kanban cards or sticky notes with task information are placed on the Kanban Board and are moved forward across the board as the task proceeds from the early stages to Done stage. This way of depicting work items on cards makes it easy for the task owner to easily share their progress just by moving the sticky note or card in the right place as the work progresses. If a card stays in one column for a long period of time, it indicates an impediment worth focusing on to ensure a smooth flow of tasks. In short, one look at the Kanban board provides a host of information to the manager regarding the progress of the project. Kanban may also place restriction on the maximum number of tasks that can be "In Progress' at any given point in time. This is known as Work Progress Limits. This helps in balancing workloads, spotting bottlenecks and ensuring optimal productivity. The Kanban board is placed in the working area of the Agile team such that it is clearly visible to the entire team. It is reviewed periodically to identify impediments, unusually long wait times and other bottlenecks. As the cards move across the board to "Done" stage, the team is free to pull new work items from the Product Backlog based on their capacity. Kanban also makes it easy to assess the Lead Time and Cycle time while drawing important insights into the productivity of the team. Lead time is the time from when a work item enters the system to when it is completed. Cycle time refers to the time taken to complete a single unit of work. While Kanban board may eliminate the need for daily stand-up meeting, it is good to have regular cadence to identify ways to improve.

A Manager's responsibility is to introduce the Kanban board to the team and make sure the team diligently updates it. There are various kinds of Kanban boards. The best is a physical board with work items represented by sticky notes. This requires the team to be co-located and working on an Agile floor. As compared to elaborate plans and status reports, it is much easier to update a Kanban board. The team should be encouraged to update it as many times during the day as needed. A co- located Agile team would usually hold their stand-up meeting in front of the Kanban board, adjusting and adding cards as the team shares their progress. However, there are many virtual boards available in case the team is distributed, eg. Trello

**Lean**

The Lean methodology is said to have become popular even before Agile started getting defined and refined. It focuses on increasing value by reducing waste. The concept of Lean originated from the manufacturing industry, but it can be applied to almost any domain, including our day-to-day life. Lean is also commonly referred to as the Lean Kaizen method. The word Kaizen means continuous improvement. For a Manager of a Lean agile team, the primary responsibility begins with identifying the key client value. A value can be any activity, task or process that directly contributes to meeting the customer needs. Very often, there is a series of activities, steps or processes needed to deliver value to the customer. This sequence of activities, steps or processes is called a Value Stream. A Tech Manager needs to map the Value Streams – analyze each step in the Value Stream to identify waste (any step or activity that is not directly adding value), eliminate waste and identify opportunities for improvement, thereby improving efficiency.

A useful tip to identifying waste is to remember the 7 possible types of waste.

**TIMWOOD**

- (T)ransportation – Unnecessary transportation of goods and material can lead to additional cost, lead time and potential damage during movement. Eg. A manufacturing plant is often built close to the source of raw material. This helps to avoid the additional cost and caution needed in moving the raw materials to the manufacturing plant.In the post-pandemic era, IT organizations are setting up their offices in Tier-2 cities where the talent lies. IT professionals no longer have to move away from their homes to work in these organizations.
- (I)nventory – Extra inventory means additional cost to hold or store them securely. Any damage or wastage of inventory means incurring cost. Eg. Keeping resources on stand-by or bench while waiting for the project to begin adds to the cost without any tangible gains.
- (M)otion – Unnecessary movement of goods, material or people may lead to additional transportation cost, potential risk of damage or accident while movement, and fatigue leading to inefficiencies. Eg. If the workplace is far away from the client site and there is a need to attend daily meetings at client site, it is better to co-locate the team with the client.
- (W)aiting – Waiting refers to the idle time of resources while on stand-by, wait time due to dependencies or pre-requisites not being met or lag between two steps in a process. This may lead to loss of productivity, delays and dissatisfaction for the client as well as the team.
- (O)ver-production – Overproduction is all about matching the supply and demand. Unnec- essary production of goods or material more than that demanded by the client results in wastage of resources and increased cost. This also leads to wastage caused by Inventory and Motion, as the extra goods or resources need to be stored somewhere which then results in incurring cost of maintaining it.
- (O)ver-processing – Overprocessing refers to the redundancy introduced in the value stream by duplicate activities like excessive reviews or providing features not requested by the client. Eg. Multiple cycles of review of any work product which has been peer reviewed once.
- (D)efect – Defect refers to the cost incurred due to errors, mistakes, oversight, or negligence.

Defect leads to poor quality, rework, and dissatisfied customer. Eg. Defects in a work product requires time and effort to resolve it, followed by another cycle of validation and verification. Once waste is eliminated from a Value Stream, the sequence of activities can flow smoothly without any bottlenecks. The team has the flexibility to exercise a pull mechanism such that work gets pulled into the value stream if, and when it is adding value.
Continuous improvement is a key ingredient of Lean methodology. Improvement is brought

about by introducing standardization and consistency, following the Plan-Do-Check-Act cycle to refine the work product and produce the best quality.The Tech Manager should also encourage the team to bring in Process improvement through innovation.

**Extreme Programming**

Extreme Programming (XP) is another Agile software development methodology. It entails very close collaboration with the customer, receiving prioritized requirements from the customer, gathering feedback as development progresses, and incorporating changes as they come in, to produce a high-quality outcome. Extreme programming leads to high customer satisfaction as the development team is almost co-creating with the customer. They are more receptive to change and develop software in much shorter cycles. Like some of the other Agile methodologies, Extreme Programming also involves iterative development, with the project being divided into short sprints or iterations. One must not confuse Extreme Programming with Scrum. The sprint cycle in Scrum is generally one to four weeks long and each sprint has a defined end objective. However, in XP the sprints are much shorter, sometimes even a few days. The team is flexible and adapts to changing requirements as per the customer needs. Features are developed, tested, and delivered within the sprint. It enables early feedback thereby minimizing any impact to the customer due to changing needs. Another key characteristic feature of XP is Test Driven Development approach. Test cases are defined before development commences. This ensures that the software that is produced is aligned with the test cases and is of good quality. Pair Programming is also commonly done in XP. Two developers work together such that one creates the code, while the other continuously reviews, provides feedback and ensures the code is improved continuously. Code from multiple developers is continuously integrated. Issues found, if any, are resolved immediately. This ensures good quality and fully functional code at all times. The code is delivered to the customer in small releases which helps the team to seek early feedback.

***Figure 2.6**: Pair Programming*

The XP development team is self-organized and has cross functional skills that help them take on multiple roles together.

**Dynamic Systems Development Method**

Dynamic Systems Development Method (DSDM) is a disciplined and structured framework for software development. Like other Agile methods, it is characterized by an iterative and incremental approach, uses time-boxed iterations with set objectives and emphasizes upon early feedback from end customer to build a quality product aligned with customer needs.

Below are some of the key characteristics of DSDM:

- Disciplined and structured framework
- Iterative and incremental development and testing
- Time-boxed iterations with prioritized functionalities
- Early inspection
- Frequent delivery
- Aligned with business needs
- Close collaboration among all stakeholders
- Empowerment of cross-functional teams
- Prototyping
- DSDM or Dynamic Systems Development Method uses prototypes to give an early view of the end result to the customer. This helps the team to get early feedback so that the product that gets built aligns with the customer requirements and provides an opportunity for refinement of requirements if needed. Hence it ensures that the outcome matches the business require- ments
- MoSCoW prioritization

The term 'MoSCoW' means Must Have, Should have, Could have, Won't have. This is a technique used for prioritization of requirements in the order - Must Have, Should have, Could have, Won't have. Most critical requirements are prioritized at the top, while the less critical ones are accommodated later as needed.

- Continuous integration and deployment
- Timeboxing
- Timeboxing is used in this methodology to manage budget and schedule. This is one of the Agile frameworks that mentions budget and schedule. While each timebox has a fixed start and end date, it helps to manage the scope along with regular checks to assess the quality.

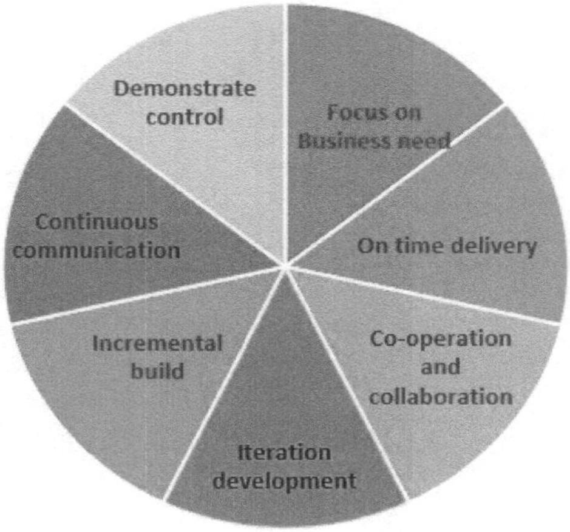


*Figure 2.7: Principles of DSDM*

**Feature Driven Development**

Feature Driven Development (FDD), as the name suggests is a framework that focuses on delivering features in an iterative and incremental manner. It has all the attributes that any other Agile methodology possesses as below:

- Requirements broken down into smaller, testable units called features
- Iterative, incremental approach
- Close collaboration among stakeholders
- Regular inspection etc.

FDD is guided by five process activities:

- Development of overall model – This is the very first step in FDD. Creation of an overall mod- el helps the team understand the overall scope and relationship between different objects.
- Creation of Feature List – The features in the overall scope are identified, prioritized, and list- ed down. This list becomes the guiding roadmap for development.
- Feature planning – A detailed plan is created for each feature. The plan captures the tasks, resource requirement and effort estimated for the feature.
- Feature design – The feature is designed, and the design is broken down into smaller, man- ageable pieces that can be independently developed and tested.
- Build Feature – The team organizes itself into smaller teams responsible for building the feature as per the design, testing it and integrating with the overall software.

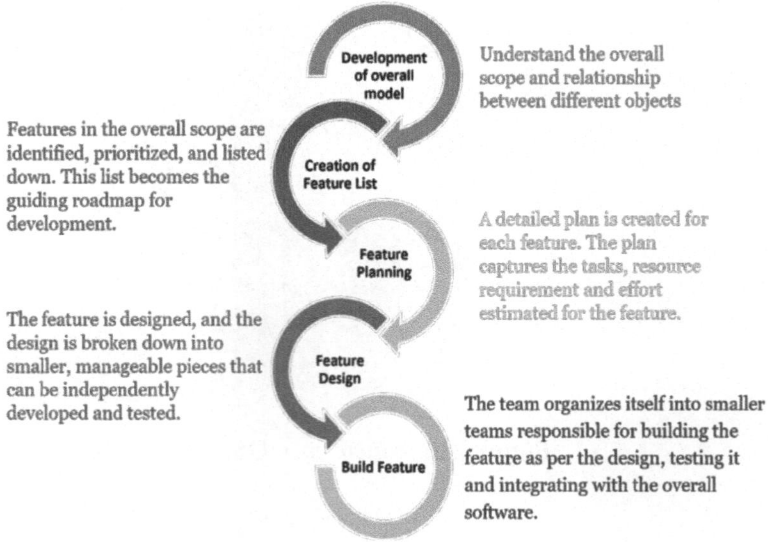


*Figure 2.8: Feature Driven Development*

### Agile Roles

Agile defines several specific roles with specific responsibilities to help the team in successfully delivering value to the customer. Below are some of the key roles defined by the Agile framework. You will notice that most of these roles align with that of the Scrum framework. Agile roles complement the pre-existing roles defined by the traditional approaches of managing project. It encourages the IT team to define their way of working and select the roles that are relevant to their project scenario.

### Product Owner

A Product Owner is the point of contact with the customer and is responsible for gathering the requirements and prioritizing them in consultation with the customer and in line with the customer's overall vision for the product. The key responsibility of the Product Owner is to maintain the Product Backlog which is a prioritized list of all the features. It is the responsibility of the PO to ensure that the value delivered by the team is maximized. The PO achieves this by diligently prioritizing and nominating features for the sprint backlog.

### Scrum Master

The first and foremost responsibility of the Scrum Master is to educate the development team on the Scrum framework. It is also their responsibility to make sure there are no impediments hindering the development team from progressing as expected and, run the Scrum ceremonies like daily Scrum Meetings etc. The Scrum master is like a servant leader to the team, helping them organize themselves, empowering them to be able to take decisions, and guiding them towards continuous improvement.

**Development Team**

The development team is a group of self-organizing, cross functional practitioners with the required technical skills who are responsible for delivering the product increment. The team collaborates among themselves to take responsibility to design, develop, test and deliver the working software. They also collaborate with the customer for early inspection, take feedback and adapt the software as needed so as to meet the customer expectation.

**Agile Coach**

As the name suggests, an Agile Coach is responsible for championing the Agile processes within the team. The agile coach continuously coaches the team on agile best practices, helping them implement them as per the project scenario and ensuring that the concepts of Agile are embraced in the true sense and the team adapts to the cultural and mindset change brought about by Agile.

**Architects**

The Architect in an agile team is responsible for creating the overall architecture and ensuring that the development team, building the work product in iterations, adheres to the design principles and makes sure that the solution is maintained and meets the requirements through the incremental development.

**Stakeholders**

Any role or individual who has the ability to influence the software being developed is a Stakeholder. This includes the customer, the management team, end users, sponsors etc. Stakeholders collaborate with the Product Owner to ensure the product requirements are understood and met, review the working software and provide feedback during Sprint reviews.

Based on the organization and the customer needs, some of the roles may be combined or additional roles defined.

**Agile Ceremonies**

Agile Meetings are often referred to as ceremonies. These meetings or ceremonies provide an opportunity to the stakeholders to collaborate better in the interest of the value being delivered to the customer.

The term "ceremonies" is akin to a ritual and a well-defined sense of purpose. Each Agile ceremony has its own significance, is outcome driven and the team shares a common understanding for them.
Some of the common ceremonies are as below:

**Sprint Planning**
Sprint Planning Meeting occurs at the beginning of the Sprint. In this meeting, the development team and the Product Owner come together to items from the Product Backlog that will be taken up for development in the Sprint. The team selects the user stories or items and then breaks down these items into smaller tasks and estimates them. The goal of the Sprint is also decided.

**Sprint Review**
Sprint review happens at the end of the Sprint. In this meeting, the development team shares what was completed and gives a demo of the working product to the Product Owner and other stakeholders. The stakeholders share their feedback, based on which the plan and priority may be readjusted if needed.

**Sprint Retrospective**
Retrospective is a very significant ceremony which happens after the Sprint review. The team reflects on what went well, what did not go well and what could have been done differently. The retrospective helps in continuous improvement.

**Daily Stand up**
The frequency of this meeting is usually daily, typically lasting not more than 15 mins. It is imperative that the meeting duration be controlled to ensure that the team adheres to the agenda strictly. In these 15 minutes, the team shares what they have accomplished since the last meeting, what they plan to do next and whether there are any impediments.
This helps the development team to synchronize amongst themselves and collaborate better.

# Summary

Agile is a flexible framework and it not only adapts itself, but also the processes and roles according to the situation. The transparency and collaboration that Agile fosters builds a foundation of trust with the customer and hence it is most suited in the present day scenario where customers are eager to be a part of the journey in building products for their business needs. Agile is as flexible and dynamic as the business itself.

In next chapter, we will cover the advantages and limitations of Agile, together with the problems encountered when following the traditional approach. We will also introduce the hybrid model and enable the learners in identifying the suitable approach to be used in different scenarios along with some examples.

# 3

# Why Agile Wins: Benefits, Limitations, and Hybrid Approaches

This chapter will give you brief details on advantages and disadvantages of Agile and in which scenario which approach can be fit and will also give insight to readers on the better understanding of traditional and Agile framework. Project management keep evolving. There are various ways of Project Management framework like Waterfall, Agile, hybrid etc. We will be covering different frameworks and decision factor for adopting the Project management methods. The requirements, circumstances of the project and the organization determine the project management approach to be used.

This chapter will cover:

- Problems in traditional approach
- Agile approach
- Advantages of Agile
- Limitation of Agile
- Hybrid Model
- Some important factors for choosing the project management approaches.

**Problems in traditional approach**

We have read the details of different type of traditional approaches in earlier chapter. These
approaches have been for a long time and have proven to be effective in many cases, but it has some limitations and drawbacks too. Traditional approaches tend to be inflexible and tend to rely more on set of procedures. This makes them not suitable for large and complex projects.

Let's looks at some common problems with the traditional approaches:

- **Rigor in nature**: Traditional approaches are more rigid, inflexible, and fixed procedure-based processes. This makes these approaches difficult to absorb the complex situations and dynamic issues that may require flexibility and adaptability. Since they are more homoge- neous solutions, they may not fit in multiple solution scenarios in the project especially com- plex engagement where one size may not fit to all the solutions. There is limitation in scope, these approaches might be well suited for certain problems but may struggle for multifaceted challenges.
- **Lack of Novelty**: Traditional approach may have lack of innovation and suppress out of the box thinking. They follow pre-defined processes, so there is little potential for new ideas. Generally, we baseline the scope and practices at initial phase of project life cycle and people follow the same.
- **Ineffectiveness in handling Complex Issues**: In today's dynamics world things changes rapidly impacting many challenges resulting in complexities. Traditional approach may not be adequate to handle the interconnected and highly complex situations, as they follow a fixed pre-determined approach.
- **Inadequacies**: In the traditional approaches there may be manual and repetitive tasks, resulting in non-productivity and wastage of resources. People often resist to changes, drivinglack of creativity to optimize resources, energy & time.
- **Lack of Data-Driven Insight**: Traditional approaches might rely more on historical model rather than data-driven insights from the current project. This can hinder decision-making in a world where data analytics and evidence-based practices are becoming increasingly import- ant.
- **Stakeholder Collaboration**: Traditional approaches works more on sequential model and individual contributors; this can sometimes discourage collaboration and teamwork. Client involvement is generally seen during requirement and testing phase or end of cycle only. This limits any course corrections in between, and in case there is a change request, it has to wait till final product is delivered, impacting in loss of effort & time.
- **Risk impact and cost of changes are high**: As product is delivered, and limited feedback mechanism at interim interval of time, any issues or defects are known only at the end. The client satisfaction score is also known at the end of cycle only. This makes the cost of any change needed as High.

### Agile approach

Today we are seeing our client priorities keep changing based on market requirements. Our process should be adaptive and flexible to absorb these changes rapidly and quickly and entertain the unprecedented level of focus on customer and consumer's needs. Agile framework provides a framework to integrate customer ideas directly into the development phase. This brings IT, business, and customers together in driving value. This not only improves customer satisfaction but also reduces the risk of project failure.

Better client experience, faster revenue streams/cash flow, reduced cost and risk all translate into higher Return on Investment, a key measurement for most of our clients.

**Key drivers for Agile transformation**
The followings are the key drivers for Agile transformation

- Fast changing business requirements.
- Improved collaboration
- Faster time to Market
- Application with direct consumer interface, periodic feedback helps in continual improve- ment and agility.
- New technology where proof points are yet to be established.

This is where Agile development makes a difference. Agile development starts with a prototype; the team works in close collaboration with the business; and short iterations ensure that team is arriving at a successful strategy as quickly as possible:

Agile business benefits can be expressed in faster revenue and cash flow due to shorter time to market; increased quality; higher customer satisfaction, reduced risk and staying within planned budge.

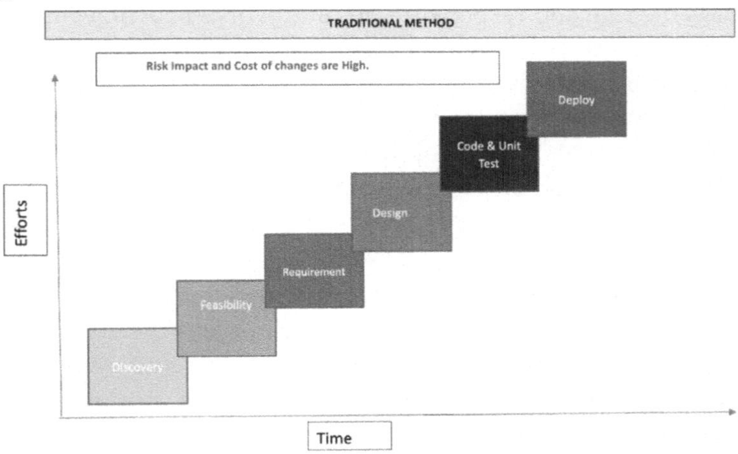


*Figure 3.1: Traditional Method*

Below image show the traditional approach showing effort versus time, which is linear sequential way of working development life cycle. Risk Impact and cost of changes are high as compared to agile approach. In Agile Development process, its faster time to market as releases arrive at the customer more frequent. It follows continuous improvement cycles, exposing risks faster. Here cost of changes is low as early detection of defects compared to traditional approach.

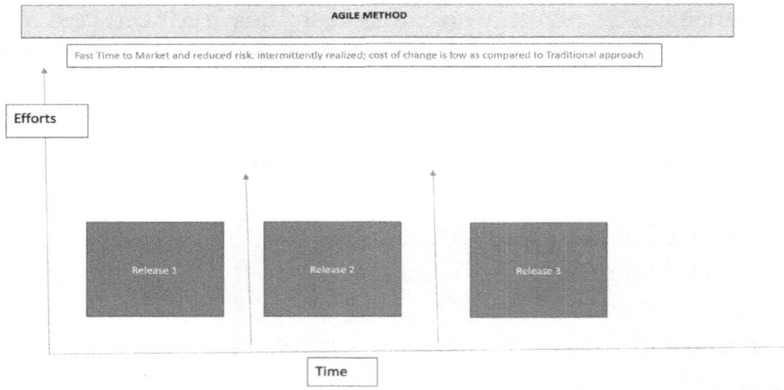


*Figure 3.2: Agile Method*

**Advantages of Agile framework**

Ability to quickly react to changing customer or competitive dynamics has become the most important competitive capability of our time. We will go through some advantages of Agile framework.

- **Continuous Customer Involvement**: Agile encourages collaboration, transparency and communication among team members, stakeholders, and customers. Everyone understands the role and responsibilities and works to achieve the common project goals. Continuous in- volvement of stakeholders strengthens the project management process. Communication is frequent and transparent, reducing misunderstandings and ensuring everyone is on the same page. This customer-centric approach enhances satisfaction and reduces the risk of develop- ing products that do not meet market demands. Complete visibility of the progress of each project in real-time. Customer, Developer, and Product Owner interact regularly to emphasize rather than processes and tools.
- **Faster Time to Market**: Agile' s iterative and incremental approach enables faster time to market. Agile promotes iterative development cycles, known as sprints or iterations. Iterative approach helps in delivering the requirement in periodic interval of time and regularly allows for quicker feedback and validation from customers and stakeholders. This iterative approach allows for early and frequent delivery of working software, which can be tested, evaluated, and improved. It also enables teams to identify and address issues or changes early in the process. This feedback loop ensures that the development team remains aligned with the market needs, leading to faster product delivery and a competitive advantage.
- 
    - **Continuous Retrospection:** It's a best practice in scrum to do Lesson learnt and retrospective after each sprint, which help in continuous improvement by strengthening the weak- ness and endorsing the positive things for upcoming sprints.

- **Flexibility**: Agile provides a flexible and adaptive approach to project management. It allows for changes in requirements, priorities, and scope throughout the project. This flexibility en- ables teams to respond to customer feedback and market demands effectively.
- **Higher Quality**: Agile methodologies emphasize the importance of continuous testing, integration, and quality assurance. By incorporating testing throughout the development process, teams can identify and fix defects early, resulting in higher-quality products. The focus on quality also reduces the risk of delivering a product that fails to meet expectations or has sig- nificant issues.
- **Risk Mitigation**: Agile mitigates project risks through its iterative approach. By delivering working increments at regular intervals, teams can identify and address risks earlier in the project lifecycle. This reduces the impact of risks and provides opportunities to adapt the project plan based on emerging challenges.
- **Self-Organized Team**: Agile methodologies promote motivated teams and emphasize individual empowerment. Team members have a say in decision-making, and their expertise is valued. This involvement increases motivation, engagement, and job satisfaction, leading to higher productivity and better outcomes.

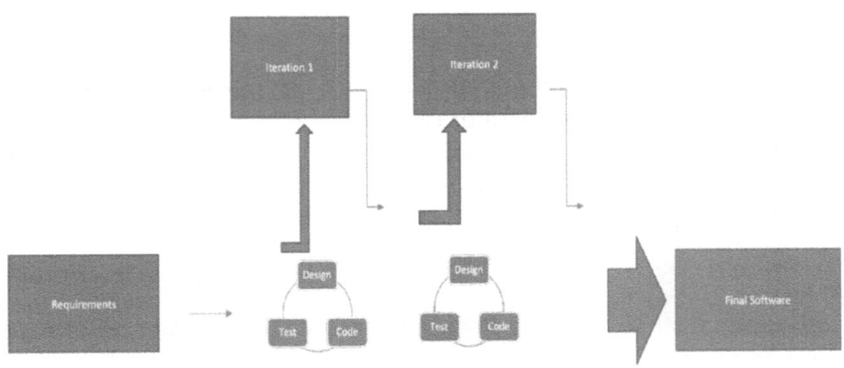


*Figure 3.3: Agile Approach*

**Limitation of Agile**

While Agile is newly evolved Project management methodologies and now widely adopted in IT industry, there are some potential limitations also to consider. It is not best fit for all the scope of work. We will learn about potential disadvantages of Agile.

- **Resistance to Change**: Employees, especially those accustomed to traditional methods, may resist Agile practices, and require time to adapt to the new way of working. This is be- cause changing the way of working from a waterfall to Agile approach disrupts the existing workflows and process in the initial phase. This may impact the productivity to some extent, but this is a temporary limitation. The gains are way more than this initial barrier.

- **Resource Intensive and complex**: Agile requires a significant investment in training,coaching, and cultural change, which can be resource intensive. The team is expected to be multi-skilled as opposed to possessing a single skill in traditional approach. Moreover, due to this reason, agile is not ideal for a fixed price contract, though can be embraced with strict discipline. Also, implementing. Agile at scale in large organizations requires coordination across multiple teams and departments which is complex to manage and challenging.
- **Overemphasis on Speed**: While Agile prioritizes speed and flexibility, there can be a risk of sacrificing long-term strategic planning and architectural considerations. There is a risk of the team losing the long-term perspective while they focus on short term goals and Minimal Viable Product (MVP)
- **Difficulty in Metrics and Measurements**: Traditional metrics may not be ideal to measure the progress in an agile implementation. Although Agile focusses on visible progress and transparency, it is difficult to measure and represent progress quantitatively. Agile metrics like Burndown Charts. Velocity graph, Cycle time etc. are designed to suit the needs of an Agile project. The team must enable themselves and get accustomed to the new ways of mea- surement and reporting through dash-boarding.

In Summary, Agile methodologies offer numerous advantages, such as flexibility, customer satisfaction, iterative development, collaboration, and higher quality. However, it is essential to be aware of the potential barriers as explained above. Understanding these advantages and disadvantages can help organizations make informed decisions when adopting Agile and mitigate potential challenges effectively.

**Hybrid Approach**

Considering advantage and disadvantages of both waterfall and Agile methodologies, Organization starts adopting the best practices from both the models based on the scope of work which emerged as the new model named as Hybrid model to create a new and better project management model. This is an approach combining elements of both traditional waterfall and agile methodologies in the software development projects.Agile project management strives for flexibility and waterfall model strives for likelihood.Below image show the best practiced from both the traditional and Agile approaches, refer as Hybrid model.

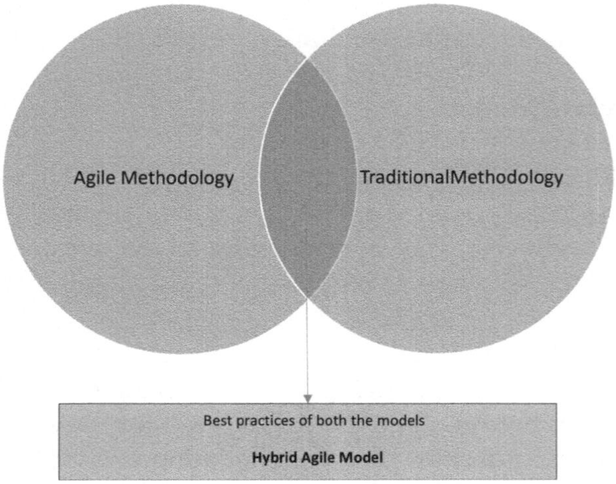


*Figure3.4: Hybrid Approach*

A hybrid approach formalizes the experimentation of using Agile in large waterfall structure, help some projects for better efficiency, quicker Innovation alongside quick schedule for others Below image shows an example of hybrid approach.

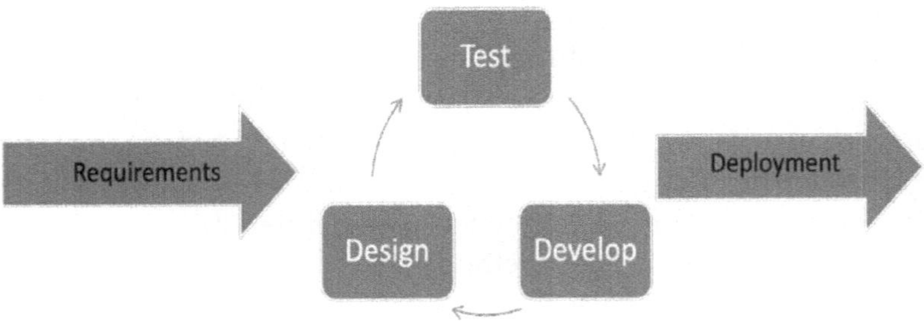


*Figure 3.5: A hybrid Approach*

Traditional approach is not speedy methodology, result will be delivered at end of the software development cycle, so it could take even months or years for customers to see final products however in Agile development is iterative resulting in shorter delivery time. In Hybrid method, plan with traditional approach, execute with Agile and helps in expedite the whole process.

In Hybrid, some examples of adoption of the processes from both the methodologies. Creating a project plan. Detailed documentation and structured approach to execute the project can be taken from traditional methodology and delivery model like iterative development, agile ceremonies like stand up, retro and self-organizing team.

**Key Features of Hybrid Model**

Below are some key features of the Hybrid model

- **Sequential Phases**: Like waterfall the project may still have defined phases, but these phases are less rigidly defined and allow for iteration and feedback.
- **Incremental Delivery**: The hybrid agile model encourages delivering working increments of the software at regular intervals, aligning with the agile principle of continuous delivery.
- **Iterative Development**: Within each phase, iterations or sprints are used to refine and im- prove the product based on feedback and changing requirements.
- **Flexibility**: The hybrid agile model allows for flexibility in change in scope, requirements, and priorities by accommodating evolving customer needs or market conditions.
- **Cross-Functional Teams**: Similar to agile methodologies, the hybrid agile model empha- sizes the importance of cross-functional teams that collaborate closely throughout the project, promoting transparency and shared ownership.
- Easy to fit compared to full agile adoption especially if teams have difficult to full y transition to Agile.
- **Feedback and Adaptation**: Regular feedback loops, such as sprint reviews and retrospec- tives, help identify areas for improvement and guide future iterations.

**Some scenarios for adopting Hybrid Model**

Below are some scenarios for which different approach/ models has been identified:

- **Large Projects**: An agile approach is best suited for small & medium sized projects i.e., smaller projects within a larger vision, while the overall Organization level vision can be im- plemented in a traditional approach with defined milestones. Hybrid approach can be used having flavor of both methodologies. It will help in structured planning and strategies and balance between predictability and adaptability.
- **Complex dependencies**: Projects with complex dependencies and fixed deadlines can work in traditional approach, with interim milestones in Agile.
- **Regulatory Requirements**: In Industries with strict regulatory compliance, such as healthcare or finance, organizations may need to adhere to certain predefined processes and documentation.
- **Fixed Contracts and Deliverables**: Project with Fixed contract and continuous change in requirements can be challenging to embrace the Agile approach. A hybrid model can give structured framework to adhere contractual requirements and allowing flexibility and adapt- ability within work break down structure and increased

development speed, lowers cost, and quick resolutions of defects

- **Geographical Distributed Teams**: Collaboration, responsiveness, ownership, coordination, and transparency are the critical pillar for the distributed team, with the blend of traditional and Agile approach we can achieve the same. The traditional project management aspects help ensure partnering across teams, while Agile practices support Ownership, collab- oration, and transparency.
- **Environments**: In the organizations where project has dependencies with Organization environment like regulatory compliance, with legacy systems or different environments, tran- sitioning to a fully Agile approach might be challenging or impractical. A hybrid model allows the organization to maintain existing systems or processes while adopting Agile practices for new or specific project components.
- **Stakeholder Management**: When stakeholders have different mindsets and different comfort level for adopting Agile. Hybrid approach helps stakeholder in adopting blend ceremo- nies and culture based on scope of work and shift left approach. Adopting a hybrid model can serve as a steppingstone, gradually introducing Agile principles and practices while address- ing the cultural shift and change management aspects.

**Some important factors for choosing the project man- agement approaches**

We learnt many Projects management framework like waterfall, Agile, Hybrid etc. Each approach has positive and negative perspectives, so it's very important to choose one that is best for the project needs.

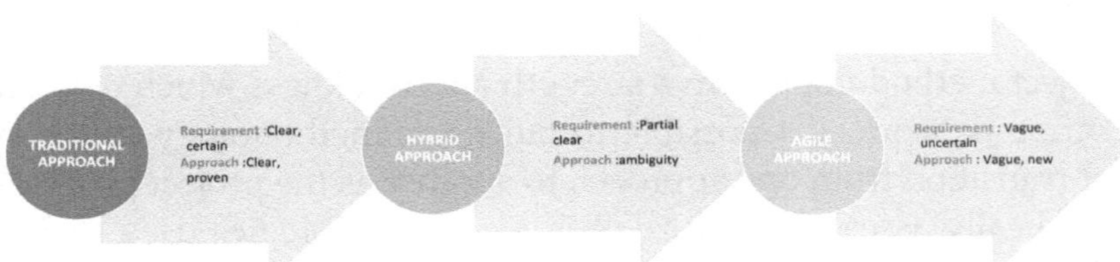


*Figure 3.6: Sample Project management Approaches*

Here are some important parameters that can guide to help which approach to adopt with sample examples.

- Understand the Project Requirements: In case only client is providing the requirement and we have dedicated Product owner - Agile methodologies can be adopted. In case we don't have any product owner and team/SME can elaborate the requirements - Driven traditional approach can be on boarded. Project scope: In case we don't have clear scope, definition or anticipate frequent change in scope -Agile methodologies can be adopted. In

case we are clear with project scope, objective, timelines, and constraints - Traditional approach can be adopted. Hybrid methods can also be used, Use traditional method for high-level planning as a kind of superstructure. use agile methods for unclear parts of the project while using traditional methods for the clearer parts.
Hybrid projects: Combination of consulting product development projects can use hybrid approach. For customer consulting work, traditional methods whereas the endeavors focusing solely on product development follow agile principles. customer wishes must be aligned be- tween the business units. Consider Project Constraints: Evaluate any external constraints that may influence the choiceof methodology. For example, regulatory requirements, contractual obligations, or industry standards may dictate certain project management practices. Consider the project budget, timeline, and resource constraints that may impact the choice of methodology especially banking projects where regulatory compliance changes frequently recommendation to use Agile methodology.

**Evaluate Project assessment**

- How is your company structured and objectives? If the project is relatively small and well-de-fined or large
- Who is end client?
- How complex is the project?
- How does each methodology risk the success of projects?
- What is size and cost of the project?
- Do internal infrastructure, technologies and processes support the methodology?
- what is team composition - offshore, onsite, vendor, client etc

# Summary

At last, each project methodologies have strength and weakness which depend upon the time and scope of work. It's possible to tailor the methodology to the specific project needs or transition from one approach to another as the project progresses.
We should periodically assess the nature of work, methodologies used and open to adjust it if required. However, frequent changes can negatively impact the process stability. There is no black and white approach, depending upon project nature, scope and objective, organization should adopt the Project management methodologies.

In the next chapter, we will learn about how to create Agile Mindset and how to being Agile,
we will be covering below topics:

- Agile Mindset
- Characteristics of Agile Mindset
- 4'C of Agile
- Practice - Doing or Being Agile

# 4

# Cultivating an Agile Mindset

The Agile mindset is a new way of thinking about work that emphasizes change, collaboration, and continuous improvement. It is essential for success in today's rapidly changing world.

This chapter will explain following topics is details the below topics:

- Understanding Agile Mindset
- Characteristics of Agile Mindset
- 4'C of Agile
- Practice - Doing or Being Agile

**Understanding Agile Mindset**

The agile mindset embodies a collection of attitudes that foster a dynamic and flexible working environment. These attitudes have respect, collaboration, continuous improvement, embracing learning cycles, taking pride in ownership, prioritizing the delivery of value, and possessing the capability to embrace and adapt to change. Cultivating this mindset is vital for nurturing high-performing teams, which in turn excel at providing exceptional value to their customers.

- Respect forms the foundation of successful teamwork. It is imperative to begin any collabora- tive effort with a deep sense of respect for one's fellow teammates. Equally vital is the recogni- tion of the significance of respect at the organizational level, extending to colleagues across all hierarchical levels, customers, and even the product itself.
- This emphasis on respect encourages an inclusive and conducive work environment, enabling teams to function harmoniously and achieve their objectives efficiently. By valuing and appre- ciating the diverse perspectives and contributions of each team member, an atmosphere of trust and cooperation is cultivated, leading to higher levels of productivity and overall team satisfaction.
- Collaboration - In the context of building increasingly complex systems and solving complex problems, it becomes impractical for any single individual to possess all the required informa- tion to complete a task effectively. Emphasizing collaboration becomes crucial in such scenari- os. By working together with other parts of the organization in a collaborative manner, the need for numerous

handoffs in the delivery process can be reduced.

- Facilitating collaboration using appropriate tools, dedicated office space, and encouraging be- havioral norms can significantly enhance the quality and quantity of collaborative discussions. When teams come together, pooling their knowledge and expertise, they can tackle challenges more comprehensively and arrive at innovative solutions. This collaborative approach ensures that the collective intelligence of the organization is leveraged, leading to improved task com- pletion and greater success in dealing with complex projects.
- Improvement Cycle - The concept of an Improvement Cycle emphasizes that no process should be rigidly fixed. Instead, every process should remain open to enhancements and refinements. In an organization that embraces this mindset, there exists a flexible approach to procedural adherence, allowing room for continuous improvement.
- By encouraging a culture that values feedback and learning from experiences, the organization fosters a dynamic environment where innovative ideas can be implemented, and adjustments can be made to optimize processes for better efficiency and effectiveness.
- The Learning Cycle encourages individuals to explore new possibilities, even if it means the possibility of failure. It provides the staff with valuable opportunities to learn and grow. In this approach, mistakes are not seen as grounds for criticism but rather as steppingstones towards progress.
- Instead of penalizing individuals for their errors, the organization offers support and recog- nition for their willingness to take risks. This supportive environment encourages a culture of continuous learning and knowledge enhancement, where each individual's growth contributes to the overall development and success of the entire team.
- Focus on Delivering Value - The primary objective of an agile team is to provide value to the customer. The team's focus should revolve around delivering what is most valuable at any given moment, and they should have confidence that they have the support of others in the organi- zation, such as managers and scrum masters, to address any obstacles that may arise. With a clear focus on delivering value, the team can prioritize tasks and projects strategically with the customers' needs and expectations.
- This collaborative approach allows the team to optimize their productivity and make continu- ous progress towards fulfilling the organization's objectives. Ability to Adapt to Change - If the customer calls two hours after a meeting, and wants changes, the organization rolls with it. Any process to manage this change can't be an impediment to the change.

**Characteristics of Agile Mindset**

The agile mindset encompasses a diverse range of characteristics, actions, and behaviors that empower individuals, teams, and organizations to achieve excellence in their performance.

At the heart of this mindset lie four fundamental pillars: flexibility, adaptability, iteration, and collaboration. These essential attributes form the foundation upon which agility is built and enable individuals and teams to navigate complex challenges, respond effectively to change, continuously improve through iterative processes. Embracing the agile mindset encourages a culture of innovation, resilience, and continuous growth, propelling organizations towards success in today's dynamic and ever-evolving landscape.

**Flexibility**

The agile mind excels in adapting to change and effortlessly navigates through various approaches to solving immediate and situational problems. This adaptability and flexibility necessitate a willingness to accommodate others, encourage a collaborative and inclusive environment. Being agile means embracing a mindset that embraces uncertainty, welcome experimentation, and diverse perspectives. By embracing change and seeking multiple paths to problem-solving, the agile mind can effectively address challenges, seize opportunities, and achieve optimal outcomes in an ever-changing world. This openness to flexibility and collaboration empowers individuals and teams to thrive in dynamic environments and drive continuous improvement, making agility an asset in today's fast-paced landscape.

**Adaptability**

The phrase "To a man with hammer, every problem looks like a nail" suggests a limited approach where one may try to solve every problem using the same method or tool, regardless of its suitability. In contrast, adaptability, which is central to an agile mind, embodies the ability to face challenges with a versatile perspective and multiple solutions. The agile mind is not bound by rigid thinking but rather embraces a diverse toolkit of problem-solving approaches. An agile mind can readily adapt to different situations, overcoming hurdles creatively and effectively. It does not get stuck on a single approach but instead explores various options to address each unique challenge. This adaptability empowers individuals and teams to navigate through complex problems and changing circumstances with ease, finding innovative solutions that suit the specific context.

By embracing an agile mindset, individuals and organizations can unlock their potential to solve problems creatively, overcome obstacles, and achieve success in a rapidly changing world. The ability to adapt and explore multiple avenues of problem-solving sets the stage for continuous growth and improvement, making the agile mind a valuable asset in any domain.

**Iteration**

Iteration, at its core, incorporate the essence of trial and error. It revolves around the process of creating better approaches to tasks and challenges by leveraging the insights gained from the results of previous iterations.

This concept embraces the value of experimentation, recognizing that not every attempt will yield the desired result, but each iteration provides valuable learning opportunities. They refine their methods, optimize their strategies, and build upon their successes and failures alike. This iterative process fosters a culture of learning, adaptability, and innovation, encouraging a relentless pursuit of excellence. By embracing the power of iteration, individuals and organizations can steadily evolve and advance, ensuring that they remain agile, resilient, and prepared to tackle any new challenges that arise. This commitment to continuous improvement makes iteration an indispensable element of an effective and forward-thinking approach in any domain.

**Collaboration**

Collaboration is at the heart of an agile mindset, as it encourages a strong and cohesive team environment where individuals work together to accomplish shared objectives. A collaborative approach emphasizes effective communication, openness, support, and transparency among team members. Communication plays a vital role in collaboration, ensuring that ideas, concerns, and information are shared openly and effectively. Being open-minded allows team members to consider various perspectives and ideas, fostering creativity and innovation. Support within the team creates a sense of trust and empowerment, enabling individuals to take calculated risks and contribute their best efforts. Transparency ensures that information, decisions, and progress are accessible to all team members, promoting accountability and alignment towards common goals. In a collaborative environment, the sum of individual contributions becomes greater than the parts, enabling the team to tackle complex challenges, adapt to changes, and achieve exceptional results. The agile mind thrives in such an atmosphere, leveraging the power of collaboration to drive success and continuous growth.

**4 C's of Agile**

When we talk about 4 C's of Agile, there are different significance of it.

4 Controls or Pillars or Values of Agile:

**Individuals and interactions over processes and tools**

- The first pillar of Agile emphasizes the utmost importance of people in the entire process. In Agile, it is crucial to prioritize regular communication with Agile teams and make each team member feel valued and appreciated as an essential contributor to the project's success.
- While processes and tools are beneficial, they should always serve as supportive assets for the teams, not overshadowing or burdening them. Agile recognizes that engaged individuals, who interact seamlessly and collaborate effectively, are the driving force behind the most successful projects.
- By fostering a culture that values open communication, respect, and recognition of individual contributions, Agile teams can achieve higher levels of motivation,

creativity, and innovation. When team members feel empowered and acknowledged, they become more invested in the project's success and are more likely to go above and beyond to deliver outstanding results.

- Ultimately, Agile's focus on people helps build a collaborative and cohesive work environment where team members thrive, enabling the organization to respond to challenges quickly, adapt to changes, and deliver exceptional outcomes.

**Working software over comprehensive documentation**

- Agile Manifesto was crafted to address the issues associated with cumbersome and documen- tation-heavy software development processes. Agile aims to streamline the development cycle by shifting away from extensive product specifications and embracing a more concise approach through user stories.
- User stories serve as compact summaries of the relevant information needed for the development process. These stories are concise, focusing on what the user needs and the value the software will provide to them. By avoiding extensive upfront documentation, Agile teams can start working on the software promptly, expediting the development process and preparing for an earlier release.
- The core idea behind Agile is to prioritize delivering a working product incrementally and continuously refining it based on feedback and iterative development. Instead of trying to docu- ment every detail before starting the work, Agile allows for flexibility, continuous improvement, and adaptation throughout the development journey. This approach enables faster responses to changes in requirements and customer needs, ensuring that the final product better aligns with the users' expectations and delivers maximum value.

**Customer collaboration over contract negotiation**

- Customer collaboration is a key pillar of Agile and stands in contrast to the traditional approach of contract negotiation. In conventional software development, customer requirements are often outlined in a legal contract before the development process starts. If the final prod- uct does not meet the initial expectations, the contract may need renegotiation, which can be time-consuming and challenging.
- In Agile, customer collaboration takes center stage. Instead of relying solely on a predefined contract, customers are actively engaged throughout the Software Development Life Cycle. They are invited to collaborate with the development team, providing their valuable input, thoughts, and potential suggestions during the product's construction.
- By involving customers throughout the development process, their feedback is directly incorporated into the software's evolution, increasing the likelihood of meeting their specific needs and expectations. This collaborative approach ensures that the end deliverable is better aligned with the users' requirements, as any changes or refinements can be addressed promptly.

- Agile embraces flexibility and welcomes customer input, allowing the development team to adapt to changing needs and priorities. This iterative collaboration results in a more custom- er-centric final product, enhancing user satisfaction and delivering greater value to the cus- tomer. By prioritizing customer collaboration, Agile fosters a customer-focused mindset and ultimately contributes to the success of the software development project.

**Responding to change over following a plan**

- As per definition Agile is "having a quick, resourceful, and adaptable character" perfectly aligns with the qualities exhibited by Agile team members. Agile team members possess the ability to respond swiftly to changing circumstances, are resourceful in finding innovative solutions, and remain adaptable throughout the software development process.
- The Agile mindset is all about embracing change as an inherent aspect of the development process. Agile teams are open to feedback, willing to adapt their software based on customer input, and continuously strive to deliver the best possible product to meet evolving needs.
- This Agile approach stands in stark contrast to traditional methodologies like waterfall, which aim to minimize change and adhere strictly to the original project plan. In contrast, Agile rec- ognizes that change is inevitable and that it can lead to better outcomes when managed effec- tively. Agile methodologies emphasize flexibility, collaboration, and continuous improvement, allowing teams to stay responsive, deliver value early and often, and adjust their course as they gather new insights.

**4 C's of high performing teams**

The beauty of being on a team is seeing people with a variety of skill sets come together to achieve a common goal. That was easier when teams were all working in the same place. While hybrid agile teams have unlocked a whole host of benefits—WFH at the hours you choose increased flexibility in how they execute the work, and more. For agile teams to truly thrive, they need better cross-functional collaboration. That can still happen on a remote or hybrid team. But companies and teams need to be truly committed to embodying the Agile Manifesto and cultivating environments where employees can experiment and fail safely.
So how do you make that happen? I'll share a few of the traits I see successful teams exhibit in their day-to-day work and initiatives that you can adopt to improve your agile team experience—no matter who's working where.

**Communication**

There can be no collaboration without communication, but that can be a serious challenge with distributed teams.

Here are a few ways to improve your team's communication:

- Disrupt the potential for isolation by "checking-in" with fellow team members at the start of the day. Once you've opened the line for communication, you'll be more likely to reach out, and so will others.

- Meet every day for standup (or daily Scrum), and possibly additional periodic check-ins at midday or end of day. By having check-ins become an established part of a routine, your team members know when to make themselves available and can better prepare updates for the rest of the team.
- Learn and use protocols for communication, including how to make decisions, how to give and receive feedback quickly, and which channels to use for different types of communica- tions. When in doubt, over communicate. Communication cuts down on misunderstandings.
- Foster a continuous improvement mindset so teams will quickly identify impediments and address them before they become unmanageable.

**Collaboration**

Collaboration is the magic that happens when people come together, interact, and create. Here are some ways to improve the magic of collaboration: Put the vision down on paper—It's dangerous to assume your team knows what its vision is. Incorporating visuals into meetings focused on things such as product development and strategic planning can also help keep everyone on the same page. By keeping the vision visible, constantly communicating about it, and keeping the team aligned, your teams will know what goal they are working towards. These moments energize teams as they work to see and build the future together. Eliminate silos by involving all of the right people in a cross-functional team that can work together to quickly deliver value. Effectiveness in collaboration increases as we cultivate human relationships. Collaboration helps people open up, offer colleagues greater transparency, and resolve conflict quickly. Collaboration is at the heart of agility, making it easy to identify new ways you and your team can succeed.

**Cultivate**

Growth doesn't happen in the comfort zone. Challenge yourself to try things in a new way. Leaders need to create a strong culture of learning—a safe-to-fail culture.
Here are some tips to start cultivating a genuine growth mindset:

- It starts with leaders. If employees don't see their leader embody this mindset, individuals won't embody it either. It just takes one negative example for everyone to begin to fear failure. Do your actions match your words? If you proclaim it to be a safe-to-fail environment where learning is valued, what do you do when an innovative program doesn't perform?
- Be transparent about goals, where the company is headed, and how the work you are doing is connected to those goals. This is a powerful motivating tool and can turn into creating some truly innovative ideas generated by a team that knows where it's headed.
- Empower individuals to make strategic decisions in their area of expertise. Don't be a bottleneck—let the people you hired do the thing they were hired to do and keep your end of the bargain by approving things quickly.

**Celebrate**

When leaders prioritize positivity and appreciation, everyone can feel the difference. One benefit of positivity is that it keeps teams engaged, which can result in a boost to morale and camaraderie. One of my favourite things is seeing the delight in a colleague's eyes when a stakeholder recognizes their efforts: it truly does make a difference. A culture of positivity is powerful. Let's appreciate and recognize one another frequently.

Here are some creative ways of doing just that:

- Celebrate wins. Get creative with this one. It can be anything from giving out coffee shop gift cards to the team to throwing an impromptu party. If your team is remote, you can hold a virtual celebration that includes a curated package sent to all attendees that will enhance the experience.
- Celebrate publicly. Tell the entire org about the fun you have and the successes you've accom plished. If there is a newsletter that goes out, ask for your team's successes to be included. If you have an org-wide Slack channel, celebrate there.

**Practice - Doing or Being Agile**

"Doing agile" refers to the practice of adopting specific agile processes and techniques, such as daily stand-up meetings, sprint planning, sprint reviews, retrospectives, and so on. It often involves implementing these practices in a superficial manner without truly embracing the underlying principles and values of agility. While these practices can help improve team communication, collaboration, and visibility into project progress, they alone do not guarantee the transformation of an organization into an agile one. Without a genuine shift in mindset and culture, the benefits of agility may not be fully realized.

"Being agile" goes beyond the mere implementation of agile processes and delves into the fundamental mindset and values that underpin agility. This approach involves a deep cultural transformation within the organization, where everyone from leadership to individual team members adapts their thinking and behaviors to align with agile principles. The core values of the Agile Manifesto, such as valuing individuals and interactions over processes and tools, focusing on customer collaboration over contract negotiation, responding to change over following a plan, and delivering working software over comprehensive documentation, guide the organization's actions and decisions.

**Challenges of Only Doing Agile**

When the teams are just "doing" agile, an enterprise can face challenges during the project development.

These challenges typically may look like these:

- When teams conduct regular stand-up meetings solely as a matter of procedure, lacking a genuine grasp of their underlying intent and essence, these gatherings frequently devolve into a mechanical exercise focused on updating status. This approach tends to address surface-lev- el particulars while failing to yield substantial resolutions. Inevitably, this undermines the very essence of the agile transformation that the enterprise is striving to attain.

- Retrospectives are often employed merely for compiling lists of issues, rather than being harnessed as effective instruments for collaboratively generating solutions and cultivating a shared sense of ownership.

A team entangled in processes and tools may lack the cognitive capacity to explore, innovate, and engage in creative thinking. Their focus primarily revolves around generating reports and completing tasks, devoid of the fervent intellectual and emotional connection with the product.

| Doing Agile | Being Agile |
|---|---|
| **Practising Agile Processes - Daily Scrums, Kanban etc.** | Agile Mindset not just following processes blindly |
| **20-30% Benefits from traditional Software development models** | More than 100% Benefits from traditional Software development models |
| **Increased accountability** | Leadership at all level |
| **Adapting & following new processes** | Learning new methods/tools for being agile |
| **Improved communication** | Employee Engagement - fun while learn |

*Table 4.1: Difference between Doing Versus Being Agile*

# Summary

In this chapter, you have learned but Agile Mindset and what are main characteristics of Agile Mindset. We learned about 4C's of Agile.

- Individuals and interactions over processes and tools
- Working software over comprehensive documentation
- Customer collaboration over contract negotiation and
- Responding to change over following a plan
- Also, we have looked at what is Doing Agile vs Being Agile.

# 5

# Leading Successful Agile Transformations

While the Agile methodology offers a swift path for software development, but success is not guaranteed. Navigating the intricate journey of Agile transformation necessitates a systematic, incremental strategy.

Wanting to be an Agile organization is different from simply following an Agile methodology within your teams. Numerous large-scale organizations fail to achieve their goals and hinder their own growth because of this. Ineffectively managed Agile transformation can lead to missed deadlines, sluggish product development, staff burnout, loss of key talent, and team conflict.

In this chapter, we will cover following topics:

- Agile Transformation Strategy
- Steps for Agile Transformation
- Agile transformation benefits
- T Shaped skill – Team

**Understanding Agile Transformation Strategy**

Agile transformation represents a substantial and intricate shift within an organization, aiming to embrace agile principles and practices across all facets of its operations. The overarching objective is to establish a more adaptable, responsive, and customer-centric entity capable of effectively addressing evolving market dynamics and delivering value to customers.

Here is a more detailed elaboration of the concept:

- **Foundation in Agile Principles**: Agile transformation starts with a deep understanding and commitment to the core agile principles. These principles prioritize customer value, col- laboration, flexibility, and responsiveness. This foundational knowledge empowers organiza- tions to make informed decisions and lay the groundwork for a successful Agile implementa- tion.

- **Leadership Alignment**: Transformation requires strong leadership support and alignment from "Chairman to Doorman" . Leadership teams must be on board with agile values and practices and demonstrate them in their actions. Leaders can pave the way for a thriving Agile environment by championing cultural change and providing requisite resources. They must drive the cultural shift and provide the necessary resources for change.
- **Cultural Shift**: Agile transformation often necessitates a significant cultural change within the organization. In order to achieve success, it is necessary to cultivate a mindset focused on constant improvement. This involves acknowledging that there is always room for growth and continuously striving to enhance one's skills, knowledge, and abilities. In order to achieve success, it is necessary to cultivate a mindset focused on constant improvement. This involves acknowledging that there is always room for growth and continuously striving to enhance one's skills, knowledge, and abilities. Empowerment, collaboration, and openness to change give teams the autonomy to make decisions and manage their work. It also means breaking down silos and encouraging teams to work together to achieve common goals.
- **Organizational Structure**: Agile organizations frequently move away from hierarchical structures to ones that support agility. Teams are organized around value streams or prod- ucts, which means that all of the people who work on a particular product or service are grouped, even if they come from different departments. Cross-functional teams bring together people with different skills and expertise to achieve a common goal.
- **Iterative and Incremental Processes**: Agile transformation involves adopting agile methodologies like Scrum, Kanban, or SAFe (Scaled Agile Framework) to guide work process- es. These methodologies emphasize iterative and incremental development, enabling organi- zations to deliver value in more minor, more frequent releases.
- **Customer-Centricity**: Agile transformation strongly emphasizes understanding and delivering what the customer truly needs. This involves gathering and incorporating customer feedback, such as surveys, interviews, focus groups, etc., into product development and regu- larly reassessing priorities to maximize value delivery.
- **Continuous Learning and Improvement**: The agile transformation journey is a never-ending journey of continuous learning and improvement. It requires a commitment to con- tinuous learning and improvement.
- **Transparent Communication**: Open and transparent communication becomes crucial during the transformation. This means sharing information, progress, and challenges with everyone in the organization.
- **Empowerment and Autonomy**: Agile teams are given the autonomy to make decisions related to their work. This means they have the authority to make

decisions about their work without getting approval from higher-ups. This empowers them to take ownership of their projects, innovate, and respond to changing conditions quickly.

- **Technical Practices**: Agile transformation often involves adopting technical practices such as continuous integration, automated testing, and DevOps to enable faster and more reliable software delivery.
- **Measuring Success**: Agile organizations use key performance indicators (KPIs) to measure their progress towards agile transformation goals. These metrics include cycle time, lead time, customer satisfaction, and delivered business value.
- **Scaling Agile**: Scaling agile practices in large organizations can be difficult, but it is possible with the help of frameworks like SAFe, LeSS, and Nexus. These frameworks provide a struc- ture for coordinating and aligning the work of multiple teams and departments.

In summary, agile transformation is a holistic and ongoing process beyond adopting a specific methodology. It involves a fundamental shift in organizational culture, mindset, and processes to become more adaptable, customer-focused, and responsive to change. Successful agile transformations require commitment, patience, and a willingness to adapt to evolving circumstances. Let us consider a small software development company experiencing challenges delivering products on time and meeting customer expectations. They underwent an Agile Transformation to improve their processes and become more customer centric.

**Key Steps and Phases of the Agile Transformation**

Agile is a new way of working that has revolutionized software development. It allows organizations to be more responsive to customer needs and to deliver products faster. Agile transformation is not a singular occurrence. It's an ongoing process demanding a change in mindset, culture, and methodologies.

Here are the key process and steps for Agile transformations:

**Leadership Commitment**

Securing endorsement and backing from top-tier leadership is mission-critical for ushering in an Agile revolution. Senior executives play a vital role in grasping the merits of Agile methodologies and advocating for change. The CEO, CIO, and top leadership recognize the need for change and commit to the Agile Transformation. They bring in Agile consultants and coaches to guide the process.

**Assessment and Readiness**

Agile coaches initially assess the organization's existing practices, culture, and readiness for Agile. Training sessions are organized for employees at all levels to familiarize them with Agile principles and practices. Provide Agile training and education to all employees, from executives to team members. All personnel, from high-ranking officials to frontline workers, must participate in Agile training and education programs. By doing so, we can cultivate a shared comprehension of Agile precepts and methodologies, fostering an inclusive atmosphere ripe for harvesting Agile advantages. To guarantee a successful Agile transition, examining the organization's present standing is crucial. This exhaustive evaluation aims to uncover its robust points, weaknesses, and level of preparation for Agile methodologies.

**Pilot Teams**

Several pilot teams are selected from different departments to experiment with Agile methodologies. In their work, these teams are given autonomy to implement Agile practices, such as Scrum. Agile coaches provide these pilot teams with ongoing support, training, and mentoring. The organization actively promotes Agile values such as collaboration, transparency, and customer focus. Leaders encourage open communication and support employees in embracing Agile principles. As the pilot teams demonstrate success with Agile, the organization decides to scale Agile practices to more teams and departments. Frameworks like SAFe (Scaled Agile Framework) are introduced to coordinate efforts across multiple teams. Pilot teams implement Agile practices, such as Scrum or Kanban, daily. They start with a limited scope to learn and refine their Agile processes.

**Transformation Teams**

We must carefully choose teams or departments to initiate a successful Agile venture. Units that boldly embrace Agile methodologies serve as a model for others to follow. Through careful identification and selection, we build a foundation of forward-thinking ambassadors who champion Agile transformation. The organization restructures its teams to be cross-functional, with members from various departments working together on value-driven initiatives. Team members are encouraged to self-organize and take ownership of their work. Teams work in short, time-boxed iterations (e.g., sprints) to deliver incremental value. Regular review meetings, like Sprint Reviews, are introduced to gather feedback and adjust.

**Customer Engagement**

Establish direct communication channels with customers to understand their needs and preferences. Customer feedback is incorporated into product development and decision-making.

**Measuring Success - Measurement and Metrics**

Align key performance indicators (KPIs) with Agile objectives, such as cycle time, lead time, customer satisfaction, and business value delivered to gauge progress effectively. Consistently track and communicate these metrics, providing actionable insights. Key performance indicators (KPIs) related to project delivery time, customer satisfaction, and product quality are established. Regular retrospectives are conducted to identify areas for improvement.

**Continuous Learning and Improvement**

The organization encourages continuous improvement, where teams regularly reflect on their processes and adjust. Lessons learned from both successes and failures are shared across the organization. Encourage teams to reflect on their processes and practices regularly. Use retrospectives to identify areas for improvement and take action to address them. Establish feedback loops at all levels of the organization to gather insights and continuously improve the Agile transformation process.

**Sustaining the Transformation**

The Agile Transformation is not viewed as a one-time effort but an ongoing journey. Leadership continues to provide support and resources, and new employees are on boarded with Agile principles. Over time, the company successfully undergoes its Agile Transformation. The organization becomes more adaptable, customer-centric, and efficient in delivering products. This transformation allows them to respond to market changes more effectively and precisely to meet customer needs. Remember that Agile transformation is not a one-size-fits-all process, and it may take time to embrace Agile principles and practices throughout an organization fully. Customization and flexibility are critical to a successful Agile transformation.

**Agile Transformation – Pros & Cons**

An Agile transformation can bring numerous benefits, but it also comes with its challenges. Here are some of the pros and cons of Agile transformation:

**Pros of Agile Transformation**

Improved Adaptability: Agile methodologies enable organizations to respond quickly to changing market conditions, customer needs, and emerging opportunities. Enhanced Customer Satisfaction: Agile practices prioritize customer feedback and collaboration, resulting in products and services that better meet customer expectations. Faster Delivery: Agile promotes iterative development, allowing organizations to deliver valuable increments of work more frequently, accelerating time-to-market. Higher Product Quality: Agile encourages continuous testing and quality assurance, leading to more reliable and higher-quality products. Increased Employee Engagement: Agile empowers teams, promotes collaboration, and provides opportunities for personal and professional growth, leading to higher job satisfaction. Transparency and Visibility: Agile practices, such as daily stand-up meetings and burndown charts, provide transparency into project progress, making it easier to identify and address issues. Better Risk Management: Agile teams identify and mitigate risks early in the development process, reducing the likelihood of costly setbacks.

Focus on Value: Agile prioritizes delivering the most valuable features and improvements first, ensuring that resources are used efficiently. Cultural Transformation: Agile transformations often lead to a more collaborative, open, and customer-centric organizational culture. Continuous Improvement: Agile encourages teams to regularly reflect on their processes and make adjustments, fostering a culture of continuous improvement.

**Cons of Agile Transformation**

- **Resistance to Change**: Employees, especially those accustomed to traditional methods,may resist Agile practices, and require time to adapt to the new working method.
- **Resource Intensive**: Agile transformations require a significant investment in training, coaching, and cultural change, which can be resource intensive.
- **Complexity**: Implementing Agile at scale in large organizations requires coordination across multiple teams and departments.
- **Initial Disruption**: Transitioning to Agile may disrupt existing workflows and processes, potentially affecting productivity in the short term.
- **Lack of Clarity**: In some cases, Agile practices may result in a lack of clear project documentation, which can be challenging for stakeholders outside the development team.
- **Overemphasis on Speed**: While Agile prioritizes speed and flexibility, there can be a risk of sacrificing long-term strategic planning and architectural considerations.
- **Dependency on Skilled Coaches**: Successful Agile transformations often rely on skilled Agile coaches and mentors, which may only sometimes be readily available.
- **Difficulty in Metrics**: Traditional metrics may need to accurately measure Agile success, making it challenging to demonstrate ROI to stakeholders.
- **Misapplication of Agile**: Some organizations may need to genuinely understand the principles, leading to a superficial or ineffective adoption.
- **Cultural Clash**: Agile principles may clash with corporate cultures, creating tension and re- sistance.

It is essential to recognize that the success of an Agile transformation depends on various factors, including the organization's readiness, the commitment of leadership, the quality of coaching, and the adaptability of the teams. Understanding the potential pros and cons can help organizations navigate the challenges and effectively reap the benefits of Agile transformation.

**T-shaped Concept & Skills**

The idea of "T-shaped skills" describes a person's ability to combine a wide range of skills and knowledge (represented by the horizontal bar of the "T") with a deep understanding and specialization in a particular field (symbolized by the vertical stem). This combination allows individuals to contribute meaningfully across diverse fields while offering valuable expertise in their specialty, making them highly valued in many professional settings. T-shaped individuals are both generalists and specialists.

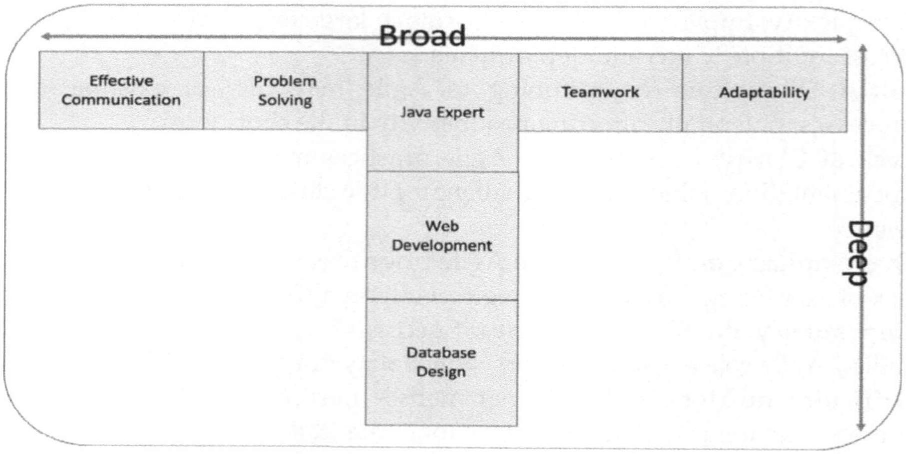


*Fig 1.1. T Shaped Skills*

Here is a closer look at T-shaped skills:

**Horizontal Bar (Broad Skills)**

- The horizontal part of the "T" symbolizes a person's wide range of abilities and knowledge. These talents include talking to people, solving problems, working with others, adapting, and knowing about several areas or fields. People who have these kinds of skills can do lots of different jobs. They are sometimes called "jacks of all trades." They can help out with lots of parts of a project or business.
- T-shaped individuals can work across different functions and are often called "generalists" because they can contribute to various aspects of a project or organization.

**Vertical Stem (Deep Expertise)**

- The " T " vertical line represents a person's exceptional expertise in a single area. That could mean they have advanced knowledge in one technical subject, field, or profession, making them stand out. Usually, this expertise is narrowly focused on one technical area, industry, or academic discipline; it also usually defines a person's principal occupation or specialty.

- Deep expertise often focuses on a particular technical area, industry, or discipline, typically representing the person's primary role or specialization.

Here is an example to illustrate T-shaped skills in a professional context:

**Broad Skills (Horizontal Bar)**

- Effective communication: Can explain complicated tech ideas in simple terms that non-tech team members and stakeholders can understand.
- Problem-solving: Capable of analyzing complex problems and finding creative solutions.
- Teamwork: A software engineer could demonstrate teamwork skills by working collaborative- ly with a team of designers to implement a new user interface design.
- Adaptability: A software engineer could demonstrate adaptability skills by quickly learning a new programming language to work on a new project.

**Deep Expertise (Vertical Stem)**

- Java programming expert: Highly experienced and knowledgeable in Java, including best practices and popular libraries and frameworks.
- Expert in web development: Specializes in front-end and back-end web development, with in-depth knowledge of technologies like HTML, CSS, JavaScript, and server-side frameworks like Spring Boot.
- Database design: A software engineer could demonstrate expertise in database design by de- signing and implementing a complex database schema for a new software application.

In this example, the software engineer possesses a wide range of general skills (the horizontal bar) that enable effective collaboration and problem-solving. However, their deep expertise (the vertical stem) lies in Java programming and web development, making them valuable contributors to projects requiring these skills. This combination of breadth and depth makes them T-shaped professionals.

T-shaped skills are highly desirable in multidisciplinary teams, as they promote collaboration, knowledge sharing, and the ability to tackle various tasks effectively. T-shaped individuals can bridge gaps between different organizational functions or departments, facilitating cross- functional teamwork and innovation.
Here are steps to help you develop T-shaped skills:

**Identify your interests and strengths**

What are you passionate about? What are you good at? Once you understand your interests and strengths well, you can start thinking about how to develop them further.

**Do not be afraid to take risks**
Stepping outside of your comfort zone is essential for developing new skills. Do not be afraid to try new things, even if you fail at first.

**Assess Your Current Skill Set**
Take stock of your existing skills and knowledge, both broad and specialized. Identify areas where you have significant expertise and where you may need improvement.

**Set Learning Goals**
Define your goals for building a T-shaped skill set. What specific skills or knowledge areas do you want to broaden (the horizontal bar), and what do you want to deepen (the vertical stem)?

**Broaden Your Skill Set**
Pursue learning opportunities in areas outside your specialization. This can include taking courses, attending workshops, reading books, and exploring online resources.
Engage in cross-functional projects or collaborations within your organization or community to gain exposure to different disciplines.

**Practice General Skills**
Develop general skills that are valuable across various domains, such as communication, problem-solving, adaptability, teamwork, and leadership. These skills make up the horizontal bar of your T-shaped skill set.

**Stay Curious and Open-Minded**
Cultivate a curious mindset and remain open to learning from different fields. Seek out diverse experiences and viewpoints to broaden your perspective.

**Networking and Collaboration**
Connect with professionals from various backgrounds and industries. Collaborate on projects or engage in discussions to gain insights and knowledge from others.

**Seek Mentoring and Guidance**
A mentor can provide guidance and support as you develop your T-shaped skills. Look for someone with the skills and experience you aspire to have.

**Continuous Learning**
Always learn new things, even after you graduate or start your career. The world is constantly changing, and so are the skills in demand.

### Apply Your Skills

Put your T-shaped skills into practice by working on projects that require collaboration across disciplines. Apply your expertise when needed and draw on your broader skills to contribute effectively.

### Reflect and Adapt

Periodically reflect on your progress and adjust your learning and development goals as needed. Be adaptable and open to refining your skill set based on changing circumstances.

### Share Knowledge

Share your expertise and insights with others. Teaching or mentoring can reinforce your deep expertise and contribute to your horizontal skills as you explain concepts to others. Developing T-shaped skills is an investment in your future. It will make you more adaptable and valuable in the workplace. It will also help you to achieve your career goals and to live a more fulfilling life.

# Summary

In this chapter, you have learned about agile transformation, how organization who aspires to become an Agile organization differs significantly from merely implementing Agile methodologies within teams.

- Also, we learnt about,
- Agile Transformation Strategy
- Steps for Agile Transformation
- Agile transformation benefits
- T Shaped skill - Team

In the next chapter, we will cover Agile framework like:

- What is Agile Framework
- Popular Agile Framework
- Choosing Right Agile Framework

# 6

# Choosing the Right Agile Framework

As you have read in the previous chapters, Agile is a concept and a mindset. It can be explained as a collection of templates, guidance and best practices. The templates are well defined methods for accomplishing tasks. Guidance is nothing but a description of approach to be followed to perform these tasks or activities. Practice, or best practices are proven ways of accomplishing some of these tasks. These templates, guidance and best practices, when put together and structured, they form a framework. This framework helps teams to understand and plan how they want to work in order to achieve their objectives.

This chapter will cover:

- Methodology vs. Framework
- Core Values and Principles of Agile
- Understanding Agile Framework
- Popular Agile Framework
- Choosing the Right Agile Framework

**Methodology vs. Framework**

Before we go deeper into understanding the various frameworks, it is important to understand what a framework actually means. We often use the terms 'framework' and 'methodology' interchangeably in different contexts. However, there is a distinct difference between the two.

Understanding the definition of the two terms is the first step towards understanding the difference between them.

- A **Framework** is a set of guiding principles that lay the foundation for addressing how a spe- cific problem may be solved. This may apply to a project, a process, or any task. It offers flex- ibility to interpret and apply the guidance in a manner suitable to the context or the problem at hand.

- A **methodology** is usually a well-defined set of steps to be followed in a given scenario. It describes the approach and techniques that can be used to accomplish a certain task. There is little or no scope to customize the procedures laid down by the methodology.

With the above definition, let us try to bring out the difference between the two:

| | Framework | Methodology |
|---|---|---|
| Meaning | The word framework means 'an essential supporting structure of a building, vehicle, or object' | The word methodology means a system of methods used in a particular area of study or activity |
| What | Framework is a broad set of principles and concepts that provide a foundation for addressing a problem | Methodology is a well defined approach comprising of detailed steps to complete a task or achieve a goal |
| How | A Framework is more flexible and can be tailored to suit the scenario. The detailed implementation is up to the user to define. | A Methodology is less flexible as it is a set of defined steps. Deviating from the steps may result in inconsistencies and may be interpreted as deviation from the process |
| When | A framework is applied when there is a complex problem to which there may not be a straightforward solution, and a need for innovative decision making | A Methodology is used to accomplish a task that has a known resolution involving a fixed set of repeatable steps to solve it |
| Example | ITIL framework, Agile, etc. | Scrum, Six sigma, etc. |

*Table 6.1 Difference between Framework and Methodology*

To summarize, framework offers a set of guiding principles that form the foundation for defining a flexible approach to solving a problem. It encourages the user to think, innovate, and make decisions appropriate to the scenario where it is being applied. On the other hand, a methodology is a step-by-step approach to solving a problem. It is more rigid in nature and is suitable in scenarios where there is a repeatable task to be performed. The choice between a framework and methodology lies with the delivery organization, its ways of working and the user depending on the problem context, scenario, and level of control required to solve the problem. It is not a one-size-fits-all kind of decision.

Every project has unique characteristics. Its complexity and uncertainty influence the choice of framework and methodology to a large extent. If the project has a lot of unpredictability, then a more flexible approach is needed. Similarly, the level of control to be exercised upon the processes also depends on the nature of the project. Another scenario affecting this choice is the nature of requirements. If the requirements are changing frequently, then an iterative approach that allows for the feature to be adapted in every iteration is desirable. On the contrary, if the requirements are well defined and not likely to change, then a more structure methodology can be defined. Every organization has its own preferred way of working which greatly influences the choice of framework and methodology. One of the reasons for such preference could be the skills and experience of the team, or the organization culture.

**Core Values and Principles of Agile Framework**

The core values of the Agile Framework underpin the thought behind the Agile manifesto. We have seen the 4 core values that form the Agile Manifesto in Chapter 2 of this book. Let us describe the values before we dive into the 12 principles of the Agile framework. The core values and the 12 principles together define the Agile framework. You will come across reference to the core values and principles of Agile at multiple places throughout the book.

**4 Core Values of Agile**

Agile has four key values that determine the way of working in an Agile framework. These values are the cornerstone behind the 3Cs of Agile - Collaboration, Communication and Commitment.

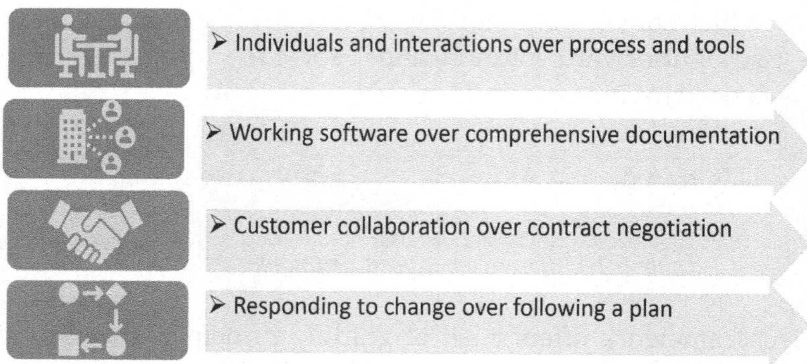


***Figure 6.1**: 4 core values of Agile*

1. **Individuals and interactions over process and tools**

Agile lays more emphasis on people and their interaction over rigid processes and tools. Agile believes that rigid process and tools limit people's thinking and curbs innovation. Therefore, it values individuals and interactions over processes and tools. However, certain project scenar- ios call for low-level processes that the team is expected to adhere to. For example, a scenario involving multiple layers of approval is required to have stringent processes in order to ensure utmost quality and stakeholder buy-in. Such a scenario should not be dealt with outside the process boundaries.

2. **Working software over comprehensive documentation**

Traditionally, documentation holds a lot of value when it comes to building any product. How- ever, as the product evolves over time with different teams adding more features to it, docu- mentation either gets left behind, resulting in something that has become obsolete over time, or hinders the evolution of the product itself in an attempt to keep pace with the product devel- opment. Agile lays more emphasis over the working software as compared to comprehensive documentation. Documentation should support the development of the evolving product rath- er than hinder its development. There are exceptions where a comprehensive documentation is a must, for example creating a user manual for a product requires detailed documentation. Hence, while Agile emphasizes on working software, it does not suggest ruling out documen- tation completely.

3. **Customer collaboration over contract negotiation**

As per the first core value, Agile always values people and interactions over processes and tools. This extends to the customer as well, and the team's collaboration with the customer is prima- ry. It encourages active collaboration between the various stakeholders, including the custom- er. This is important to make sure that the customer is engaged in the overall development and is giving continuous feedback. This kind of collaboration is more important as compared to negotiations over the contract. It helps in making sure that the team is able to build a software that meets the customer expectations. However, there may be situations that call for contract negotiation to be necessary. An example is a scenario where multiple vendors are working on an engagement with strict Service Level Agreements. In this scenario, contract negotiation is crucial.

4. **Responding to change over following a plan**

Agile emphasizes on flexibility and responsiveness to change rather than following a stringent plan. It is important to embrace change and adjust the plan as needed during the development of the software to make sure that the end product that is created meets the requirement and emerges as the best possible end product. On the other hand, Agile does not absolutely rule out following a plan. If the situation demands, and stakeholders hold the team accountable for any deviations, then it is required to follow the plan and document the deviations.

**12 Principles of Agile**

The four core values are supported by 12 key principles of Agile. The figure below gives a quick recap of the key principles that drive adherence to the core values.

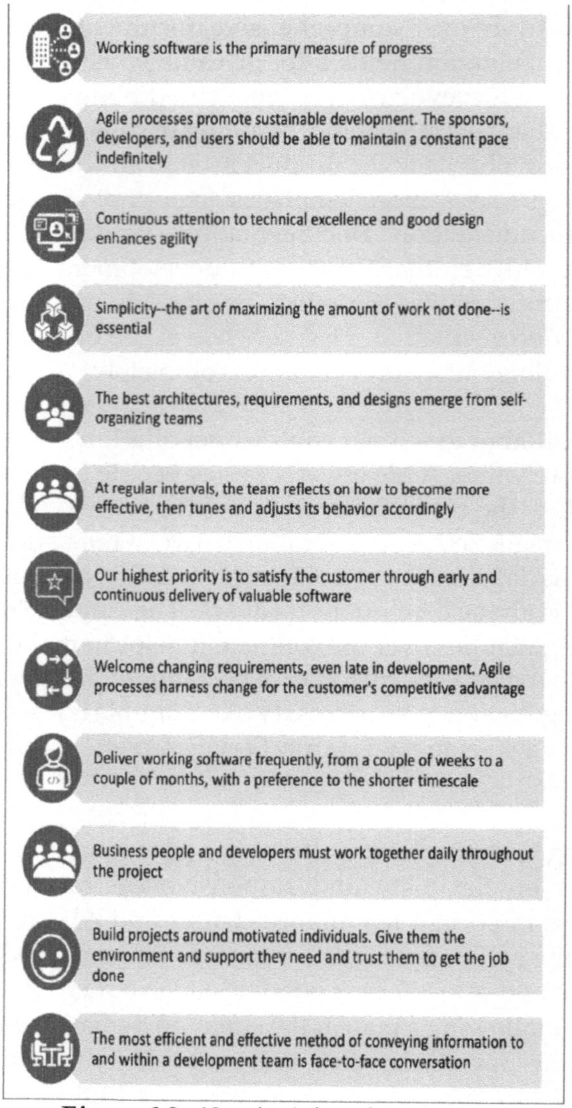


***Figure 6.2**: 12 principles of Agile*

**Understanding Agile Framework**

Agile framework is a structured approach that establishes how to operate in an Agile environment. This includes managing and executing projects, building products, or creating visible and useful outcomes for the client. Though Agile framework is typically popular in the IT industry, it is not uncommon to see other industries also adopting and following Agile way of working in various ways and to different degrees, while embracing the principles laid down in the Agile Manifesto (refer Chapter 2).

You may recall that the Agile Manifesto lays emphasis upon the following set of values:

- Individuals and interactions over process and tools
- Working software over comprehensive documentation
- Customer collaboration over contract negotiation
- Responding to change over following a plan

The key objective in an Agile framework is to deliver value to the client in a fast manner and be flexible and responsive to changing requirements.
The key features of Agile framework revolve around the Agile manifesto and support the manifesto in various ways. Described below are the key features. Read and understand how each of these features play a significant role in strengthening the Agile manifesto.

**Iterative and incremental Development**
The overall product is broken down into smaller pieces, each being a working unit and independently testable. Development happens in incrementally, with each iteration adding to the functionality of the work product developed so far, until all features are added and the product is ready as a whole. Each iteration allows the work product to be inspected, and feedback, if any, is incorporated, and the work product is adapted till it meets the customer requirement.

**Collaboration with the customer/Customer-centric approach**
In an Agile framework, the development team and the client walk together in the overall journey of developing the end product. There is very close collaboration with the customer with frequent feedback loops that help create a product that is close to perfection.
The customer-centric approach places the customer at the center and ensures that the product is built to the customer's satisfaction by being responsive to change and making sure that the customer has a competitive edge in the dynamic market with the product that is built for them.

**Flexibility and Adaptability to change**
An Agile team is open to accepting any change in priorities, requirements or plans. The team focuses on short term goals, adjusts the plan, and adapts the software according to the feedback so that the end product that is created matches with the customer expectation. It is natural for new insights to emerge, leading to change. The team is responsive to such changes and ensures that plans are adjusted continuously, even if the change is late in the cycle.

**Cross-functional teams**

In order to provide a more holistic approach, it is imperative to have close collaboration amongst the various stakeholders. This helps to reduce delays due to dependencies across teams. All stakeholders bring together different aspects of the project or product as a whole, thus enabling faster resolution of inter-dependencies, thereby promoting faster progress.

**Continuous Improvement**

Iterative development with close collaboration with the stakeholders enables having multiple and frequent feedback loops. As the team incorporates the feedback, they work towards achieving a more refined and better-quality end product by adopting the principle of continuous improvement.

**Transparency**

Having open communication around progress, challenges, improvement opportunities and success helps to increase transparency amongst the various stakeholders.

**Frequent Deliveries**

Small sprint cycles creating a working software results in frequent deliveries. Frequent deliveries is also a result of close collaboration coupled with multiple feedback loops. Incorporating this feedback in order to improve the product leads to frequent deliveries. Eventually, this enables continuous improvement.

**Retrospective**

Agile teams hold regular retrospective meetings amongst them to discuss and reflect upon their processes, identify areas of improvement and make adjustments to their way of working to resolve problems that have occurred in the past.

**Minimum Viable Product (MVP)**

A minimum viable product is a minimal version of a software or product that, when delivered, demonstrates essential and working features which can be reviewed by the customer and feedback can be given.

**Sustainable pace**

Agile promotes a constant and sustainable pace as averse to over-work, stress and burnout of the team.

**Face to face communication**

Face to face communication allows teams to capitalize not just on verbal communication, but also the tone, expression and body language. There is better clarity and alignment amongst the team members, which leads to faster resolution of issues and queries, faster decision-making, and better alignment and understanding amongst them. There is better collaboration and alignment of thoughts.

**Emergent requirements and design**

Agile acknowledges that it may be difficult to foresee what the end product should look like and define the requirements accurately in advance. Hence, Agile is open to embracing change even if it arises late in the development. By doing so, it creates room for requirements and design to evolve as the project progresses.

**Self-organizing teams**

Agile teams are empowered to make decisions on key requirements, design, and architecture-related matters and take complete ownership of the work.

**Continuous Integration and continuous delivery**

Agile encourages teams to make use of CI/CD pipelines to ensure the code being written is getting continuously built and integrated with the rest of the code and is also continuously getting deployed. This helps to ensure that the code being written is error-free and that development and testing are taking place rapidly.

**Continuous feedback**

Continuous feedback from the customer and the team forms the basis for development of a work product that meets customer expectation and is of the best quality. The Agile team collaborates closely with all stakeholders, including the customer, and seeks regular feedback on the working software, the process as well as on the iteration gone by through retrospective meetings. This helps in continuous improvement.

**Time boxed iterations/Sprints**

In the Agile framework, the project is divided into multiple smaller cycles or time boxes, usually up to 4 weeks in duration. This short cycle is referred to as Sprint or Sprint Cycle. Requirements are broken into smaller features, and features form the scope of a Sprint. This mechanism of breaking down the product into smaller chunks is very useful when the product is complex. It helps the team to understand the Product and build it bottom up gradually. These time boxes also become the basis for planning, execution, and review.

**Test Driven Development**

Many Agile teams follow the practice of writing the tests before development of the software. The compliance of the developed functionality or code against the requirements is then validated through the tests written beforehand. This is called test-driven development.

**Prioritization and Value Based Planning**

The Agile team bases its prioritization on the customer needs and the business objectives. It prioritizes and adjusts its plan as per the feedback from the customer and changing business priorities. Requirements, broken down into features as the unit of development are ranked in order such that the most important features are developed and delivered first. Business drives priority, and the order of tasks depends on that.

**Popular Agile Frameworks**

Agile Frameworks and methodologies is one of the most frequently discussed topics, be it the difference between framework and methodology, or the examples for the same. You have learned to differentiate clearly between the two (refer section Framework vs Methodology in this chapter). You have also learned the various Agile Methodologies (refer to Chapter 2).

Agile frameworks have gained popularity in the industry due to various advantages they offer over the traditional project management which follows a linear path.

**Agile means Speed, coupled with Adaptability**

For Technical Project Managers, the most significant advantage that Agile offers over the traditional framework is the speed at which work progresses. The project team has complete freedom to prioritize and re-prioritize their work unlike the traditional approach that is very rigid. Because of the rigidity, there are dependencies that are not met on time and therefore a delay is caused. The critical path becomes longer since work happens sequentially based on a plan that was created without full visibility. On the contrary, Agile enables the team to adapt as they move, ensuring that the end product is what the customer expects. Hence the team not just produces outcomes with speed, but also adapts it as per the customer expectation equally faster.

**Relationship with the customer is easy and collaborative**

The team builds a good relationship with the client since they start collaborating from the beginning. If there is any change in priority or direction of work which may cause delay, customer buy-in is already there. Hence the Manager does not have to do the difficult task of convincing the customer on the reasons for delay or change. At the same time, it is also easy for the customer to introduce a high priority change at any point in time without having to enter into negotiations on impact of change on cost, schedule and effort.

**The project team is a happy team**

Since the agile team including the customer work together towards the project objective, there is no need for difficult conversations if there is any event causing change in schedule, objectives etc. The customer buy in is always there since the customer is part of the Agile team too. This makes the job of the Project Manager very easy.

**Progress is visible and transparent**

Since Agile teams work in short sprint cycles that result in demonstratable progress, the roadmap for the entire project is visible to all stakeholders at all times in a transparent manner. The stakeholders have the freedom to introduce change at any point in time while they also understand the impact of the change. This makes it easy for the Project Manager to manage change.

**An Agile team is a healthy team**

The Agile frameworks are structured such that the team does not burn out in their attempt to meet deadlines. Hence there is less stress. The customer gets an opportunity to give feedback on small demonstrable features and user stories being developed in every sprint. Hence the customer is confident that the end product will meet the overall objectives. Several frameworks have gained popularity due to their ease of adoption and flexibility they offer. Agile has become a culture and a way of working and is a mindset more than a framework now. In this section, let us identify some of the well-known and most frequently used Agile Frameworks and understand why they have gained popularity.

**Lean Agile Framework**

Lean agile development has been inspired by the manufacturing industry - one of the oldest industries. The manufacturing industry has a keen focus on eliminating waste. The same principles have been adopted by several industries including Software Development and maintenance in the IT industry. It is referred to as Lean Agile Development.

We have seen a description of the Lean wastes in Chapter 2 (remember TIMWOOD). Here is a quick recap:

- (T)ransportation
- (I)nventory
- (M)otion
- (W)aiting
- (O)ver-processing
- (O)ver-Production
- (D)efect

Minimization of these wastes lead to optimization of the processes. Lean is a key ingredient of most Agile methodologies. Lean framework was influenced by Taiichi Ohno, Shigeo Shingo, and others from the Toyota Production System.

As a Manager, one of the key objectives is to manage and minimize the cost of the project. In order to minimize the cost, traditionally, there has been a pressure on the teams to deliver more in the same time. As a result, teams are often stretched on time, and under pressure to over-work.

Lean brings a different perspective to look at how cost can be minimized. In any project lifecycle, there are many operational and transactional tasks which do not add value to the end product directly, eg. Loads of documentation that grow obsolete over time since nobody has the time to keep updating them as the product evolves. This is an opportunity for the Agile project manager to eliminate such tasks that do not add direct value. A Technical Manager can divert the time and effort spent in such activities towards activities that add direct value to the end result. This is a very easy and efficient easy to maximize productivity of the team without adding undue pressure or crunching the timelines. The Technical Manger needs to simply focus on identifying tasks that can be eliminated to free up the bandwidth of the team.

In a Lean framework, the foremost thing to do is to define what brings value to the customer. Anything that does not add direct value, is considered to be waste and is recommended to be eliminated.

An easy way to define value is to create Value Streams, that represent end to end steps, tasks, activities, resources and processes needed to produce an end result. The Value Stream depicts the flow of work and gives the manager an opportunity to identify non-value adding activities, unnecessary dependencies and bottlenecks that cause delays and eliminate them for the team to be more productive.

Once the delay causing wastes are eliminated, the Technical Manager must ensure that there is an un-interrupted flow of work for the team. The Technical Manager must also ensure that the development of features is prioritized by the customer's demands, rather that the team's ability to develop features. The scope of each sprint is driven by the market demands thereby exercising a pull system rather than a push. This helps the manager to eliminate the waste related to excess Inventory or Over-production. The Technical Manager must use a Just-in-Time approach to deliver features as they are needed. There is a risk of introducing inventory cost if the features are delivered in advance. Lean is often also referred to as the 'Lean Kaizen' approach, meaning it imbibes the culture of Continuous Improvement. The manager along with the team is encouraged to keep identifying small improvements that add value to the customer and the work product. This culture of continuous improvement is inherent in Lean approach.

The Value Stream mapping exercise is one of the ways to identify small improvements, opportunities to standardize certain approaches and processes and build a future state that is more optimized, has reduced waste and aligns well with the customer expectations. The entire Lean team participates in this mapping exercise and gets an opportunity to voice their concerns, observations and suggestions. This helps the Manager in creating a future state that is more acceptable to the team and adds more value to the customer. This exercise is also a good lever to develop team bonding, mutual understanding and respect.

The Lean Agile Framework can be easily applied to not just the IT industry, but also other industries. The principles of Lean Agile are easy to understand and practical. It helps the team to think logically and progressively to weigh each action and determine if it is adding value or not. A team that is convinced of the value their actions are adding to the customer, is a motivated and successful team! This makes the Lean Agile framework a popular framework adopted across industries.As a Technical Project Manager, if your focus is on eliminating waste and introducing continuous improvement, think Lean!

**Large Scale Scrum (LeSS)**

We have seen a detailed description of Scrum in **Chapter 2**, **Large Scale Scrum uses principles of Scrum** as well as some additional practices to roll out Scrum in a scenario where multiple teams work on the same product.

***Note***: *This framework was created by Craig Larman and Bas Vodde.*

Large Scale Scrum involves scaling Scrum to large organizations. Scrum is a very well-known Agile methodology. Imbibing Agile practices in the entire organization is a huge task and involves a huge amount of coaching, mentoring and cultural change. Scrum, these days is almost synonymous with Agile. With the growing adoption of Scrum by various project teams across the organization, it is easy to scale it to the entire organization and become the obvious choice.

Large Scale Scrum uses the core principles of Scrum (refer Chapter 2) and extends it to complex projects and across the organization. It is flexible and lightweight and involves working with multiple Scrum teams on a complex project.

Scrum at scale does not introduce any new principles or roles. It fundamentally uses the Scrum roles of Product Owner, Scrum Master and Development team collaborating on ceremonies like Sprint Planning, Daily Scrum meeting, Sprint Review and Spring Retrospective to achieve the objectives of a larger organization.

A single Product Backlog is shared by all teams that helps to maintain transparency across teams. A uniform 'Done Criteria' is applied across the teams to ensure consistency in quality of deliverables.

The Technical Manager needs to ensure that his/her team participates in a common Sprint Planning exercise that is carried out across the teams in a coordinated manner. The single Product Backlog is used as an input to the planning exercise. During this Sprint planning process, inter-dependencies are brought to notice and handled in a collaborative manner. The Tech Manager collaborates closely with other teams to make sure that the product is aligned with the end goal of the organization or the complex project. This builds a sense of ownership and inclusion in the larger team and helps the team as a whole to focus on the product and the customer. This is a product-centric approach with the customer as the focal point.

This framework is extremely powerful in case of a large or complex project where it is difficult to achieve incremental, fast and visible progress with a single scrum team. It offers the advantages of transparency, flexibility, adaptability and retrospection, and at the same time is flexible and can be adapted to suit the needs of the larger organization. It helps in adopting the Agile culture and way of working across the organization.

As a Technical Project Manager, if your focus is on scaling Agile practices across the organization while still being flexible, think LeSS.

**Disciplined Agile Delivery (DAD)**

Disciplined Agile Delivery is a framework that brings together various Agile and Lean approaches. By doing so, it offers a framework to teams which allows them to choose and select the practices that are suitable to their scenario. Hence, though the name indicates 'disciplined', this framework is more flexible and gives the flexibility and guidance to select the practices and tailor Agile according to the context in which it is being applied. In short, the team defines its own 'Ways of Working'.

***Note***: *This framework was created by Scott W. Ambler*

The key differentiating factor of DAD is that it brings together Agile practices across the full software development lifecycle starting from inception, architecture and design, construction, testing, deployment and operations. It takes a holistic view of the entire lifecycle to make sure all aspects of software and solution delivery are catered to.

DAD also provides several different lifecycle approaches and practices like Agile, Lean etc. to the Tech Manager. The Technical Project Manager has access to a wide variety of lifecycle approaches and practices. The manager has the freedom to select, deviate and tailor processes as per the project needs.

DAD defines a wider set of roles such as developer, tester, designer, Product Owner etc. Each role has a well-defined set of responsibilities that add up to create a full delivery process. It also defines project Phases and milestones which are very similar to a traditional way of project planning. This makes it very easy for traditional project managers with little or no exposure to Agile, to adopt this framework. However, this framework embraces DevOps which encourages continuous development and delivery to production in a frequent and seamless manner. Like any other Agile framework, DAD teams possess hybrid skills to be able to contribute effectively to all phases of the project lifecycle.

If you are a Technical Manager with not much exposure to the Agile methodologies, this is a good framework to get started. It allows you the freedom to select the approach and practices suitable to your needs, enabling you to easily transition into the Agile practices at your own pace.

**Scaled Agile Framework (SAFe)**

SAFe is a framework for scaling Agile to large organizations, imbibing the roles, practices, and principles to coordinate work across multiple teams in an organization in an attempt to align them with the organizational goals. It helps enterprises in applying a structured set of practices across multiple complex project teams, extending up to the entire organization. This framework was created by Scaled Agile, Inc. It embraces the core principles and values of Agile and Lean, like transparency, continuous improvement, customer-centric approach and alignment.

There are four levels at which SAFe can be applied. Each level has a set of roles associated with it to help achieve the objectives at that level.

- **Team level**: This is the level where individual teams work at a project level. This is a typical cross functional Agile team. The Team level roles are similar to Scrum, with Scrum master and Product owner being the key roles of the cross functional team.
- **Program level**: At this level, multiple teams come together within a program to deliver a larger solution for the Program. At this level, new roles get introduced – Release Train En- gineer (RTE), Product Owner and Scrum Master for better collaboration and co-ordination. The RTE plays a very critical role in coordinating the various activities at the Program level between various Agile teams working together towards the end goal. The RTE has the primary responsibility to ensure everything runs smoothly. SAFe typically comprises of 5 to 12 Agile teams (Agile Release Train - ART) working together at Program level to deliver value. Syn- chronization between these teams is absolutely important, and this is where the RTE role is critical.
- Release Train Engineer is the chief Scrum Master for the Agile Release Train whose key re- sponsibility is to keep the train on track by facilitating the Program level events and removing any impediments that hamper progress.
- Product Owner, Program or PO-Program maintains and prioritizes the Program Backlog and works with the different teams to prioritize features.
- System Architect provides the Program level design and architectural decisions and makes sure that the team aligns with the enterprise level architectural guidelines.
- Scrum Master, System or SM-System has the primary responsibility to co-ordinate activities amongst multiple teams on the Agile Release Train and make sure there are no impediments.

- **Large Solution level**: At this level, multiple Agile Release Teams work together on complex value streams to deliver a complex value. Solution Train Engineer has a significant respon- sibility of coordinating between multiple Agile Release Trains to make sure they deliver the larger solution.
- Solution Architect provides architectural direction to the multiple ARTs on the larger solu- tion.
- Release Management coordinates and manages the releases and dependencies to make sure that the overall solution is delivered. Portfolio level: This is the highest level where strategic planning happens across various complex value streams.
- Portfolio SAFe (PSA) is the highest leadership role in SAFe, responsible for aligning the port- folio with the organization's strategic objectives.
- Epic owner prioritizes epics based on strategic objectives and goals.
- Enterprise Architect provides oversight to ensure all value streams are aligned with the strate- gic enterprise architecture.
- Value Stream Engineer manages value stream activities, ensures value delivery and alignment with strategic objectives and goals.
- Lean Portfolio Management manages financial and strategic aspects of the portfolio and en- sures that it aligns with the strategic objectives and goals. The above four levels show how Agile practices get scaled starting at the team level, and right up to the organization level.

**Choosing the right Agile Framework**

For a Technical Project Manager, it is important to select the right processes, practices, methods and tools for the project. This selection is done at the start of the project. It is not enough to just make the right selections. The methods, processes and practices should also be socialized with the team to ensure that the team understands the project management framework, agrees and believes that it is the right framework to meet the project objectives and is enabled to follow the framework appropriately. Educating the team and aligning them to the selected framework is key to the success of the project.

Before making any decision or choice, the Technical Project Manager must base the decision on the key principles of effective decision making. Decisions are often not perfect, hence there should be a scope to be flexible so that if anything goes wrong with the decision, there is a means to adapt your choices without compromising the goal. Flexibility in this case is almost synonymous with agile.

- **Understand the decision problem**: To choose well, you need to understand the decision problem - in this case, understand the project and the organization. Understanding the project and the organization becomes key to choosing the appropriate framework.

- **Identify the objective**: To make sure that you have selected the right framework, ensure that the chosen framework helps you in achieving the end result, in this case, the stakeholder needs. The entire team, along with the Technical Project Manager must be clear of the project goals and objectives and align with the customer so as to meet their expectations.

- **Weigh your options**: Often while embarking on a project, the Technical Project Manager is presented with multiple alternatives. Make sure you study the alternatives, identify the pros and cons of each before you decide. A smart way to go about this is to look at other similar projects, go through learnings and best practices and industry standards and benchmarks. Talk to managers who have led successful projects using different frameworks and learn from their experiences and failures. Once you have done this, take a decision based on your key criteria for selection.

    - **Learn from experience**: Consult the experts who can not only help you understand your project context before you make a decision, but also in educating you and your team on some of the suitable frameworks relevant to your project scenario. In short, reflect, learn, improve and proceed Below are some of the important activities that will help you in choosing the right framework. Understand the project and the organization. The goals and objectives of the project, the scope, size, complexity, regulatory requirements, measuring criteria are important things to under- stand. In addition to that, the organizational culture, team skills, processes are other factors to consider when doing a due diligence to select the right framework.
    - Stakeholder needs. Carefully understand the stakeholder needs, identify the key stakeholders, their priorities, level of influence and expectations.
    - Define the key criteria for selection. Identify the influencing factors, prioritize them, and define the criteria that will influence your decision-making.
    - Evaluate team skills. Some frameworks may require specific skills. Make sure the team is edu- cated on the principles of the Agile framework. Engage the right mix of cross-functional teams. If needed, it is good to train the team, as well as the customer in some cases before engaging them on the project.
    - Pilot the framework. If there is a lack of any compe
    - lling factor to choose a specific framework, it is good to pilot the framework on a small piece of the scope. Reflect on the experience of the team before finalizing the framework.
    - Consult experts. Do not hesitate to consult with experts when in doubt. Engage an expert to get you started on the project.
    - Reflect, learn, improve, proceed. Even after a framework has been chosen, reflect on the team's experience, learn from your mistakes, look for opportunities for improvement, and proceed forward with a motivated and experienced team.

# Summary

Agile offers many different methodologies and frameworks to choose from. No matter which framework or methodology you proceed with, the core values and principles of Agile remain the same. Agile offers immense opportunities to customize your way of working to suit the needs of the customer, the organization and the team. The key point is to have a motivated and self-directed team that is empowered to make decisions, evolve the design, and be responsive to changing customer expectations.

In next chapter, we will cover Agile in the IT and non-IT world and its benefits. We will also learn about the Agile habits the team must inculcate, the challenges faced in embracing Agile, and SMART (Specific, Measurable. Achievable, Relevant and Time-Bound) tasks that help to overcome all hurdles and succeed.

# 7

# Agile Across Domains: IT and Beyond

This chapter will give you brief details on the benefits of adopting agile and what are the core challenges we faced while implementing the Agile with the mitigation approach. We will also discuss the implementation of Agile in non -IT world and the significance of SMART tasks in Agile world.

This chapter will cover:

- Benefits of going to Agile
- Understanding S.M.A.R.T Tasks
- Agile Habits
- Various ways to apply Agile in non-IT organizations
- Core Challenges in implementing Agile.

**Benefits of going to Agile**

Agile project management primary focuses on delivering maximum business values and priorities. It can be implemented in both IT and Non -IT industries. In today's evolving world, business keep changing rapidly impacting to increase in adaptability to business requirements. Embracing an agile approach will empower businesses to stay competitive amidst rapidly changing technology and market trends. It gives more control to the product development team, visibility to client and flexibility to the management.

Here we will discuss some benefits of going to Agile compared to traditional approach.

**Accelerate Time to Market**

With the Agile approach, we work in an iterative nature and time box way. Releases are split into sprint; industry standard of each sprint cycle is 2 weeks. This continuous delivery approach, accelerate the deployment faster to market providing a competitive edge over the competition. This also allows organizations to get early market feedback and deploy useful features and capabilities faster, giving them a larger market share.

**Early and Ongoing Customer Validations**

Agile methodologies embrace change, empowering teams to adjust to changing requirements, market circumstances, and client feedback. By consistently evaluating and adapting to change and by regularly reviewing and adjusting priorities aligning with client stakeholders and consistent feedback, Agile teams can respond to new insights or challenges without many issues. This improves the overall success rate of projects and client satisfaction. Agile methodologies prioritize customer collaboration and feedback throughout the development process. It accelerates the adaptability and flexibility.

**Increased Transparency regarding Project Development**

Transparency is crucial for fostering trust, collaboration, and accountability. Agile promotes transparency by agile ceremonies, tools and processes. It promotes open and clear communication channels within the team, keeps stakeholders involved throughout the project. provide them with regular updates, involve them in key decisions, and address any concerns they may have promptly. Agile makes decision-making processes transparent and ensures tha decisions taken during sprint planning or other meetings are communicated to the entire team, providing insights into the project's direction. Conducting regular demo sessions to showcase completed work to stakeholders, not only provides transparency into the team's accomplishments but also allows for immediate feedback. Agile methodologies provide for an open culture and transparency for the deliverables for all the stakeholders. Issues/ defects are captured in collaborative tools like JIRA, Trello boards, etc. using Agile ceremonies like stand- up meetings, retrospectives, etc

**Early Identification and Prevention of Defects**

Clearly define user stories with well-crafted acceptance criteria. Helps in setting expectations and understanding the requirements thoroughly, reducing the likelihood of defects due to misunderstanding. Implementing continuous integration practices helps to merge code changes frequently. CI systems automatically build and test the application, providing early feedback on integration issues and defects.

**Reducing Risk and Improving Quality**

As mentioned above Agile helps in Early identification and prevention of defects, help in reducing risks and improved quality of deliverables. Agile project management techniques reduce project risks as the work is split into smaller chunks and undergoes frequent reassessments. This proactive approach reduces the probability of any major setbacks or failures as the potential issues are identified early and can be resolved by the team.

**Enhance Group Spirit**

Increased team ownership is encouraged by agile rather than individual contributor. It empowers team members by trusting them to make decisions within their areas of expertise.

Trust is a key factor in building a positive team culture and enhancing group spirit. Celebrate team successes, whether they are small achievements during a sprint or major project milestones. Recognizing and appreciating collective accomplishments boosts morale and reinforces a positive group spirit. It also increases team ownership, collaboration, and morale. By embracing and adopting Agile, organizations can reap benefits, enabling customer satisfaction, adaptability, collaboration, minimizing risks and higher-quality deliverables.

**Understanding S.M.A.R.T tasks**

The idea of SMART tasks is frequently used to define the work that needs to be completed within a specific iteration or time frame in Agile methodologies like Scrum or Kanban. These SMART tasks adhere to the SMART goals' guiding principles, but they are used in a more tactical and iterative setting. Agile tasks that are SMART typically refer to user stories or tasks that are:

- **Specific**: The requirements for each task should be well-defined and clear. There should be no ambiguity and an articulated and understood focus and scope.
- **Measurable**: The task should be able to be tracked as it is being completed that is at any given point, we can quantify the % completion. Examples include metrics like time spent, fea- tures used, or other pertinent quantifiable measures.
- **Achievable**: The task must be doable and realistically achievable within the iteration. It should consider the skills of the team, its capabilities, activities that can be controlled or in- fluenced, available resources, and external considerations that may impact the tasks' comple tion.
- **Relevance**: The task must be directly related to the sprint's or iteration's current goals and objectives. It must also enhance the overall worth of the thing being created or move the pro- gram toward the overall objective.
- **Time-bound**: Each task should have a specific deadline for completion, which is typically the length of the sprint or iteration. Planning and prioritization are aided by this.

**Agile Habits**

While delivering in an Agile framework, individuals and teams adopt certain behaviours, practices, and principles that are referred to as "agile habits." These habits contribute to the development of an agile, collaborative, and continuously improving culture.

Here are a few typical Agile practices:

- **Iterative**: Agile teams focus on small increments of work over the iterations (sprints). This allows them to continuously improve their work, get feedback, and alter based on the same.
- **Collaboration**: Agile has a strong emphasis on collaboration between team members, stake- holders, and clients. Effective communication, feedback, and Knowledge sharing allow for open and transparent information sharing.

- **Flexibility**: Agile teams are open to change and are ready to adjust the plans in response to changing requirements. The plans are progressively elaborated instead of being cast in stone.
- **Transparency**: Agile promotes openness in all aspects of delivery, team members commu- nicate their successes, setbacks, and progress regularly to improve trust and decision-making. Every team member is involved in daily/periodic scrums and is aware of the status of the project.
- **Customer-Centricity**: Agile teams focus on the business needs of the clients and workclosely with the product owners. This allows the team to be focused on the client's needs with greater focus.
- **Constant Learning and Improvement**: With an iterative approach, Agile facilitates a culture of continuous learning and development. Teams can frequently evaluate their actions and outcomes to improve productivity and effectiveness.
- **Empowered Teams**: Agile teams are self-forming and self-organizing. They can control their work and activities and are empowered to make decisions.
- **Feedback-Driven Development**: Agile relies on consistent feedback loops, such as sprint reviews and retrospectives. Teams use criticism and constructive feedback to constantly im- prove their work.
- **Value Delivery**: Agile teams prioritize the features based on their importance and use to the end client. This allows the teams to optimize the value delivered to the end clients.
- **Regular Communication**: Agile ceremonies enable regular communication amongst the team, client, and other stakeholders. This helps move faster in a more open and transparent environment.
- **Cross-Functional Skills**: Agile is effective when the team members have diverse skills. The team members are encouraged to have a variety of skills.
- **Visual management**: Agile teams frequently use visual tools like task boards, burn down charts, and Kanban boards which provide a visual real-time status to all stakeholders.
- **Continuous testing and Test-Driven Development (TDD)**: Agile teams develop test cases before writing code to ensure quality and speed up testing and deployment.
- **Time boxing**: Agile tasks are split into fixed periods, like sprints. This enables predictable governance and allows for real-time decision-making.

These Agile practices support a culture of adaptability, collaboration, and value delivery and help Agile methodologies be adopted and implemented successfully.

**Various ways to apply Agile in non-IT organizations**

Originally, IT corporations were the target audience for it this development of Agile frameworks. However, it is not exclusive only to the IT industry; non-IT organizations can also use and benefit from it. The following are some key factors to consider while implementing Agile in non-IT organizations.

**Educate team about Agile values and principles**

Ensure all team members should understand the Agile manifesto, principles and values and tailor the practices based on the industry scope of work. Ensure that teams receive adequate training in Agile principles and practices and transitioned to an Agile mindset. For example, iterative models could be used across industries, making a movie can be implemented in Agile way, with iterative small releases and identify and incorporated area of improvements in agile way.

**Client Centric approach**

Identify all the critical Internal and External stakeholders, create and understand work backlogs and prioritize the identified tasks based on client value. Translates the vision into a set of features and an expected time box in which to deliver them. It is also important to define the roles and responsibilities. This can be implemented across any industry.

**Adapt to change and Flexibility**

Be adaptable and open to change when organizing your project. Non-IT sectors could encounter changing market conditions, in which case Agile's flexibility might be a big benefit. Changes can be released in the iterative manner based on client prioritization. Adopt Agile Habits We have covered Agile behaviours in detail above. These practices ought to be adopted by non-IT organizations as well, given their work scope and priorities.

**Ensure that your Agile cycles are stable and predictable**

Establish sprints or fixed-time iterations to establish a task delivery cadence. This promotes regular retrospection and modification and helps to establish predictability.

**Cross functional team**

Form cross-functional teams by assembling individuals with a range of industry-relevant talents. This encourages collaboration and a thorough approach to problem-solving. Promote teamwork and knowledge sharing to increase productivity and efficiency.

**Continuous Improvement**

Agile encourages ongoing development. Get feedback from stakeholders and team members on a regular basis to find areas that need improvement. Establish a foundation for integrating automation and innovation. This can be implemented in any industry. Agile principles have been successfully implanted outside of the IT and software development industries. Agile concepts have been adopted by many industries, including manufacturing, marketing, education, and even healthcare, to enhance their operations and results.

**Some Examples of Agile in the Non-IT industry**

Agile can also be implemented in Non-IT industry, followings are the few examples to implement Agile in Non-IT industry:

- **Project management**: Agile principles can be useful for non-IT projects as well. To increase efficiency and adaptability, teams break projects down into smaller tasks, prioritize them based on value, and deliver increments frequently.
- **Product Development**: Agile can be used to develop prototypes, gather user feedback, andmodify offerings based on customer input whether creating tangible products or services.
- **Marketing**: Iterative planning, testing, and adaptation of marketing campaigns are features of agile methodologies like "Agile Marketing." Marketers continuously improve their strate- gies based on feedback and data.
- **Education**: By enabling teachers to modify their lesson plans and curriculum in response to student feedback and performance, agile principles can be used to modernize education.
- **Healthcare**: Agile principles are being investigated to improve hospital operations, enhance patient care, and foster a patient-centric approach.
- Large-scale production runs, protracted lead times, and a concentration on the continuous production of a single product were common characteristics of traditional manufacturing processes. Customer preferences and market conditions can, however, quickly alter in the dy- namic market climate of today. Some creators have adopted Agile concepts to adjust to these changes and stay competitive.
- Agile manufacturers construct prototypes or minimal viable products (MVPs) quickly and use them as testbeds for obtaining input from customers and stakeholders rather than investing significant time and resources in designing and producing a complete product. In Summary, Agile concepts may be effectively applied in a variety of industries, including manufacturing, to increase flexibility, customer focus, and adaptation in the face of shifting market condi- tions. Agile principles are not just confined to IT.

**Key Challenges in implementing the Agile and mitigations steps**

During the implementation of Agile, there may be challenges that could be roadblocks for various tasks. In this section, we will discuss such challenges and their mitigation steps.

**Lack of Stakeholders commitments**

While moving from traditional to Agile approach. People resist within organization to shift the approaches. We have seen many gaps identified in the agile transformation with respect to stakeholder commitments, addressed below. Lack of Client commitment and product ownership. Without support from top management, Agile transformations may face roadblocks. Lacking a vision and strategy for the product roadmap. Not having Product owner from client side. Lack of collaboration with client, business, and vendor scope creep across and within iterations Low quality of user stories Inadequate handoffs and handshakes between the technical teams.

**Mitigation Steps**
Gradually introduce Agile practices, starting with small, incremental changes. Encourage open communication and collaboration. Educate leadership about the benefits of Agile methodologies. It's important to change the stakeholder mindsets Involve executives in the Agile transformation process. Establish clear communication channels between teams and leadership. Align Agile goals with overall business objectives. Have dedicated product owned, Product roadmap strategy and vision. The principles of INVEST (Independent, Negotiable, Valuable, Estimable, Small and Testable) should be applied while evaluating the Caliber of user stories. Estimation approach and assumptions should be aligned with client. Reward and acknowledge actions that are consistent with the Agile values. Established ground rules that are in line with team members should be made and followed. Roles and responsibilities ought to be established and carried out.

**Absence of ONE TEAM culture**
Existing organizational culture may not align with Agile values and principles. People believes in individual contributor than team contribution.

**Mitigation Steps**
Introduce Agile methods gradually, making tiny, gradual changes with visibility of roadmaps. Encourage open communication and collaboration. Team collaboration and involve in part of decisions making, build as "one team". Provide continuing guidance and assistance. Promote the use of tools like certificates, mentorship programs, and workshops.

**Inadequate attention to process improvement and learning**
Absence of a thorough retrospective. Nothing deliberate has been done to support continual delivery.

**Mitigation Steps**
Each sprint should end with a retrospective, and subsequent sprints should adhere to the lessons learned. The course of action should be the development lifecycle's automation; automated testing; continuous integration, release, and deployment; and appropriate handoffs and handshakes between the technical teams

**Inadequate metrics and governance**
Failure to implement crucial agile metrics. Lack of a definition for "done" and acceptance criteria. No coach for Agile actively. No routine evaluation of Agile maturity.

**Mitigation Steps**

Implement robust Agile project management tools (e.g. real time soft copy of storyboard) for transparent communication and governance. Onboard key Agile metrics and govern them for continuous improvement. Onboard Agile coach for proper guidance. Agile maturity assessment should happen periodically to identify gaps and work on action item for better maturity.

**Team working from remote locations**

Team working from different locations.

**Mitigation Steps**

When not in colocation, put in a lot of effort and consider innovative ways to mimic colocation. Create a foundational toolkit for communicating. Document Exchange/Talks/minutes of meetings Common Discussion Boards, Files, and Guidelines Video conference calls. Every day, there should be a minimum of one handshake meeting between onshore and offshore personnel. Ground rules should be established and followed.

# Summary

Agile principles can be used in both the IT and non-IT worlds, depending on the scale of the project. Client happiness, reduced risk, efficiency, improved predictability, and communication will all benefit agile can be adopted. Many industries, including manufacturing, marketing, education, and even healthcare, have embraced agile concepts to improve their processes and outcomes. Agile methodologies promote communication, openness, and continuous learning in both IT and non-IT situations. We also learned key challenges in adopting Agile with mitigations.